REPEAT
On this Side

Line of Panel & Door

Face of Pres Marble Jamb.

(4' 11½" Stone to linoleum.)

Face of Jamb. of Metal Door.

Ed Door.

Repeat on
this Side

Repeat On other Side

REVISED DETAIL OF DOOR JAMB.
Scale ¾"=1'-0"

ALL STONE WORK TO BE EXECUTED UNDER SUPERVISION OF ARCHT
ALL MEASUREMENTS TO BE VERIFIED AT JOBS.

AIL OF PANEL "E" F.S.

MEMORIAL
LIBRARY
W. H. RATCLIFF
ARCHITECT
CHAMBER OF COMMERCE BLDG.
BERKELEY, CALIFORNIA

THE ARCHITECTURE OF RATCLIFF

The Architecture of

RATCLIFF

WOODRUFF MINOR

PHOTOGRAPHY BY KIRAN SINGH

Heyday Books   BERKELEY, CALIFORNIA

FOR SAM AND DOROTHY
in domo Patris mei mansiones multae sunt

Library of Congress Cataloging-in-Publication Data
Minor, Woodruff.
The architecture of Ratcliff / Woodruff Minor ;
photography by Kiran Singh.
p. cm.
Includes bibliographical references.
ISBN 1-59714-042-2 (hardcover : alk. paper)
1. Ratcliff Architects. 2. Radcliffe family.
3. Architecture—California—San Francisco Bay Area—
20th century. I. Singh, Kiran, 1951- II. Title.
NA737.R296M56 2007
720.92′2—dc22
[B]   2006013389

Cover Art: Kaiser Medical Center, Fresno, 1994. Façade detail.
Frontispiece: Mason-McDuffie Building, Shattuck Avenue, Berkeley, 1929. Sculptural capital.
Cover Design: David Bullen Design
Interior Design/Typesetting: David Bullen Design

Orders, inquiries, and correspondence
should be addressed to:
Heyday Books
P. O. Box 9145, Berkeley, CA 94709
(510) 549-3564, Fax (510) 549-1889
www.heydaybooks.com

Printed in Singapore by Imago

10 9 8 7 6 5 4 3 2 1

Contents

Foreword

Every generation is born to a legacy. Whether they yield a privileged way of life like our own or the dire toll on the environment our children will inherit, legacies entail both opportunity and challenge. At the century mark of Ratcliff, I am keenly aware of the values that have sustained our firm and the challenges ahead as we work to cease disruption of Earth's systems and find harmonious interaction with nature.

The Architecture of Ratcliff came to be because of the idea that there was something vital and interesting about the personality of this company and the guiding values informing the buildings, events, and individuals of Ratcliff and the Bay Area. By reflecting on our past and articulating our experience, we hoped to find useful insights about the path ahead.

My grandfather and father were lucky men: given skills and opportunity, each thrived in the time and place of his lifetime. They chose to be architects, to be ethical in their dealings with people, to bring zest to their habits of work and play. Each headed an enterprise that engaged a great number of women and men over the years, and they left us a legacy replete with loyal clients and a portfolio of earnest and often beautiful buildings conveying the aspirations of their inhabitants.

They also represented the last generations to perceive the earth as having inexhaustible resources. While they revered nature and cherished the forests, oceans, and mountains, they enjoyed the abundance of land and materials that so richly appointed the buildings we treasure today.

The values and passions that guided the firm then are still relevant and useful: architecture remains very much an act of optimism and reverence when spaces are designed to serve and delight generations to come. Our firm's architecture continues to integrate physical elements in artful and holistic ways to meet our clients' needs and dreams. Our firm remains, in the words of Peter Scott, who was president in the 1980s, "honest and open, unassuming, intellectually eclectic and curious." This is our legacy as a firm and as architects.

Yet we can no longer ignore the paradox of architecture and the built environment's role in depleting earth's resources and destabilizing our climate. The challenge we face is to design in ways that ennoble the human spirit while reversing the terrible toll on the earth wrought by our heavily populated civilization. In our generation, architects, clients, and governments have led the way in learning to design sustainably, and we celebrate the beauty of this new architecture that better supports Earth's systems. It is a good opening chapter to our future, and no other challenge comes close in importance to working to restore our planet.

THINKING about our centennial and being a part of the making of this book have been instructive and enjoyable. I am grateful to Woody Minor for synthesizing reams of archives and project records into an eloquent, rigorous analysis of the firm's place in the broader realm. I have enjoyed Kiran Singh's friendship and can see his vitality reflected in his beautiful photographs. A high point has been the collaboration with publisher Malcolm Margolin and the gifted individuals from Heyday Books he assembled for this project.

Seeing the span of the firm's history alongside the saga of professional evolution and societal change is rejuvenating as we move into a new century with a clear mission and strong foundation. At its core, I believe Ratcliff will remain a firm where architects bring forth a humane world in healthy balance and in deep resonance with time, purpose, and place.

Christopher (Kit) Ratcliff
March 2006

Introduction

This book is the story of Ratcliff, the San Francisco Bay Area's oldest architectural firm. Since 1906, the company has had an unbroken strand of leadership over three generations in one family. The story moves forward from father to son to grandson, or it delves back from son to father to grandfather, depending on your point of view.

The firm's founder, Walter H. Ratcliff, Jr. (1881–1973), came to California from England in 1894. His father, a clergyman and teacher, moved the family to Berkeley several years later so his three children could attend the University of California. The town was fast becoming a center of architectural achievement, exposing the young man to an array of work that set him on the path to his career. Following graduation from the university in 1903, with no formal training in architecture, young Ratcliff worked and apprenticed in the office of campus architect John Galen Howard, studied in Europe, entered into a short-lived partnership in San Francisco, and then established the practice in Berkeley that would be the focus of his fifty-year career. The firm dates its birth to March 15, 1906, when Walter H. Ratcliff, Jr., received license no. 388 from the state of

California. He soon took his place among Berkeley's well-known coterie of architects, including Maybeck and Morgan, initially as a designer of Arts and Crafts houses and ultimately as an exponent of revivalism, deploying a variety of styles on a wide range of commercial, civic, academic, and ecclesiastical commissions. From its zenith in the 1920s, when the firm's work included major projects for the Pacific School of Religion, Mills College, and Berkeley's downtown, the early practice declined to more modest levels during the Depression in the 1930s and World War II in the 1940s, surviving primarily through the efforts of its sole employee, Scott Haymond.

Walter Ratcliff's oldest son, Robert W. Ratcliff (1913–1998), a graduate of the School of Architecture at the University of California, Berkeley, joined the firm in 1945. To the new partnership (Ratcliff, Haymond & Ratcliff), he brought the modernist sensibilities of mid-century America. Working with his father in the 1950s (Ratcliff & Ratcliff), and with his partners Murray A. Slama and A. Burns Cadwalader in the 1960s and 1970s (Ratcliff, Slama & Cadwalader), Robert oversaw the creation of an office with a new identity derived not only from its modernist approach to design but also from its expanding sphere of activity in northern California and a widening range of projects that included hospitals and civic centers. What had been under the father primarily a Berkeley firm became under the son a regional one. Enlarged to five partners and renamed The Ratcliff Architects, the office thrived in the 1980s with health care and academic work throughout

California, and it received recognition for an innovative terminal at Oakland International Airport.

Robert's oldest son, Christopher (Kit) Ratcliff, a graduate of the UC Berkeley College of Environmental Design, became CEO in 1987, bringing a more holistic approach to the practice. The 1990s were a time of transition, involving a move to Emeryville, a merger, and new partners. In 2000, bearing a shortened new name (Ratcliff), the firm entered the twenty-first century with prospects as bright as at any time in its history.

It is the burden of this book to demonstrate how Ratcliff has managed to outlast all other architectural offices in the San Francisco Bay Area. What has it achieved over the past century, and how does it fit into the broader context of architecture in America? The firm provides a fascinating study in continuity and change, combining the stability of multi-generational family ownership with the dynamism of an evolving culture and the practice of architecture within that culture. As one engages with the story, it soon becomes clear that the professional virtues of integrity, excellence, and service are at the heart of Ratcliff's tenacity. The broad path of mainstream architecture has always been the domain of skilled practitioners who have produced the majority of durable designs in our towns and cities. Yet historians and critics often overlook this important body of work, focusing on the brightest stars at the expense of the wider field of vision. This narrow view has impoverished the profession by failing to take into account the very qualities that imbue not only buildings with longevity and lasting value, but the firms that create them as well.

Architecture is an endlessly complex subject whose meaning has been endlessly debated by theorists, historians, practitioners, and critics. I have used the classic formulation "firmness, commodity, and delight" as a perceptual grid to help me understand and appreciate the buildings in this book. A building can be admired, even adored, from any of these perspectives. If it is built well, with structural integrity and fine materials, it can be loved for its "firmness." If it serves its human purpose well, with imagination and grace, it can be loved for its functional "commodity." And if it imparts some sense of truth and beauty—those most elusive and debatable of qualities—a work of architecture may become a work of art, transcending its context with timeless "delight."

The architectural ideal in this formulation is the integration of firmness, commodity, and delight into a seamless whole, wherein each is simultaneously itself and the other—not a well-built structure lacking functional or visual grace, nor a highly functional building that is shoddily assembled or ungainly in appearance, nor a beautiful building with a leaking roof and perverse plan: rather, a building whose structural and functional qualities are inseparable from its aesthetic and emotive power: all in one, one in all, a three-part unity not unlike the classic theological concept of the Trinity. The reader would do well to bear this formulation in mind while encountering a century's worth of Ratcliff architecture.

THERE are many people to thank. Like a building, a book such as this is a team effort, and to attribute the finished work to one person is to distort the truth of the creative process. As the writer, I depended on the work of numerous scholars; on the informed advice of many colleagues, whom I have endeavored to name; and on the technical and artistic support of editors, designers, and photographers. *The Architecture of Ratcliff* grew organically. Its provenance is rooted in Berkeley's artistic traditions. In the 1920s, when Walter H. Ratcliff designed the new Fine Arts Building at Mills College, the Oakland women's college where he served as campus architect, he made the acquaintance of Roi Partridge, an art professor married to the photographer Imogen Cunningham. The two families became friends. Roi and Imogen's son, the Berkeley photographer Rondal Partridge, produced hundreds of images of buildings for Robert Ratcliff and his partners in the 1950s and 1960s (some of which are reproduced in this book). In the 1970s, one of Rondal's daughters, the writer Elizabeth Partridge, married Robert's son Tom, Kit's younger brother. In 2001, Elizabeth and her sister Meg created a book of their father's photography published by Berkeley's Heyday Books, the publisher of this volume as well.

It has been a personal privilege working with Heyday. To publisher Malcolm Margolin and editor Jeannine Gendar, heartfelt thanks for their initial encouragement and abiding patience. Art director Rebecca LeGates, designer David Bullen, and photograph consultant Lois Brown collaborated on a beautiful product. And it has been a pleasure working with Kiran Singh, the photographer whose images enrich the book; we spent many hours together looking at buildings, making room for some memorable meals along the way.

To be invited to immerse oneself in the life of a company is to be given a rare opportunity. Despite the seriousness of its business and the busyness of its schedule, Ratcliff opened its doors and made me feel welcome. How can I possibly list all the people there who contributed to the making of this book? I can only begin by thanking Kit Ratcliff for his unwavering green light and engagement, which ignited my drive and kept me moving. Elizabeth (Liz) O'Hara was there from the beginning, guiding the book forward to completion. If Kit was principal in charge, Liz was project manager, and this book is theirs as much as anyone's. Many others at the firm helped me gain a deeper understanding of the human, technical, and artistic dimensions of a modern architectural office, and I list them with gratitude: Heidi Bilodeau, William Blessing, Gary Burk, Crodd Chin, Kyle Chin, Rose Cowperthwaite, David Dersch, D. Roger Hay, Miyo Itakura, Cheryl Lentini, Susan Martin, Steven McCollom, Thomas Patterson, Arnis Silarajs, Carolyn Silk, Molly Skeen, Richard Steele, Dan Wetherell, Bill Wong, Robert Wong, Chellene Wood, and publicist Mary Tressel.

I had enjoyable and informative conversations with former principals Syed V. Husain, Donald T. Kasamoto, and Peter Gray Scott, and with Scott's wife, and the firm's former business manager, Teresa Ferguson; with Burns Cadwalader's widow, Barbara; with Scott Haymond's daughter, Christine Kramer; and with former staff designer Jules Kliot. Family members Walter H. Ratcliff (youngest son of Walter H. Ratcliff, Jr.), Lucy Ratcliff Pope, Walter W. Ratcliff, Kenneth E. Ratcliff, Thomas T. Ratcliff, and Janet Tam also took the time to speak with me.

The research files, map collections, tour booklets, and other publications of the Berkeley Architectural Heritage Association were essential to documenting the career of Walter H. Ratcliff, Jr. Particular thanks to BAHA's Anthony Bruce, Susan Cerny, and Lesley Emmington Jones for their expert assistance. Gary Goss contributed information from his meticulously researched files on Bay Area architects; Kevin Frederick gathered data from immigration and census records, city directories, and newspapers; Michael Adamson's review of state and local records elucidated the origins and operations of Alameda County Home Builders, Inc., and the Fidelity Guaranty Building and Loan Association. Previous documentation by Kenneth E. Ratcliff (on the Ratcliff family history) and by Nicholas Hanson and Walter W. Ratcliff (on the career of Walter H. Ratcliff, Jr.) proved invaluable. Donald Andreini and William Beutner of San Francisco Architectural Heritage and Betty Marvin of the Oakland Cultural Heritage Survey shed light on buildings in their cities. The staffs of the Bancroft Library, College of Environmental Design Library, Berkeley Public Library, Berkeley Historical Society, Oakland Public Library, and California Genealogical Society and Library all gave of their time.

Thanks are also due to the many homeowners,

churches, schools, and businesses that gave access to their buildings and archives. Special thanks to Terry Dyonzak, Director of Facilities at the Pacific School of Religion, Berkeley, and Paul Richards, Director of Campus Facilities at Mills College, Oakland, for their unstinting cordiality. Rondal Partridge, Meg Partridge, and the Imogen Cunningham Trust of Berkeley freely opened their collections (and memories) for perusal.

Finally, my gratitude to those individuals who took time to read and respond to drafts in various stages of completion—Sharon Gallagher, Michael Corbett, Susan Cerny, Annette Sandoval, and Ward Hill. Among my readers at Ratcliff, Roger Hay was of particular help in the final stages. Caffeinated conversations with friends at Vine's and Jay's cafés, memorably with Robert Kimball, Richard Knight, and Dawn Jurasin, helped the words keep coming. Dad, David, and Mark were always there for me, and so was Sharon. Thanks to you all.

Woodruff Minor
April 2006

The Architecture of

RATCLIFF

One   The Ratcliff Heritage

WALTER H. RATCLIFF, Jr., came of age at the end of the nineteenth century, a period of profound reassessment and reform in the practice of architecture.[1] To progressive reformers, the era's architectural legacy seemed like cacophony—discordant buildings and disharmonious cities strewn across a violated landscape. The proponents of classicism, led by the Ecole des Beaux-Arts in Paris, sought to impose order through rational planning and a balanced approach to design inspired chiefly by the example of the Renaissance. The English Arts and Crafts movement delved further back in history, deriving its ideals from the communal, naturalistic, pre-industrial vernacular of the medieval world. Classicists and medievalists alike wished to remold their society, and both looked to the past for inspiration; to varying degrees, both were "historicist." Progressive architects of the period worked primarily within one or the other of these reform traditions, often blurring the boundaries between the two.

This is to say that Ratcliff belonged to the last generation of architects to believe in the power of precedent to meet the needs of contemporary culture. He assimilated the reform-minded tendencies of his day, giving his work a seriousness that has helped it to endure. He was both representative of his time and somewhat atypical: for an architect of his caliber, his career had rather unusual origins. He would enroll at the University of California before there was a school of architecture and teach himself how to design houses as a speculative business venture; his later training would be limited to several years of employment/apprenticeship and a few months of schooling during a European tour. Yet his practice came to exhibit confidence in

Arts and Crafts neighborhood on Piedmont Avenue, in Berkeley's Elmwood district.

its handling of architectural solutions in a remarkably short time.

The historicism Ratcliff practiced had deep roots. Since the Renaissance, architects had been plundering the past to reinvent the present, refashioning precedent in the perennial search for truth and beauty. At the continental Ecole des Beaux-Arts, then the world's most prestigious school of architecture, students were taught to draw from the well of classical reason, while the Arts and Crafts movement, spreading outward from England to Europe and America, imparted a more intuitive and archaic sensibility—a distinction that today might be characterized as left-brain and right-brain awareness. The vanguard of the profession in the United States in the late nineteenth century was largely composed of Ecole graduates who were also conversant in the Arts and Crafts mode. (Typically, their more public commissions followed the precepts of the former; residential work tended toward the latter.) Their efforts gave rise to an increasingly refined architecture of eclecticism, one that sought to evoke the past with suppleness rather than literalness. Historians would label this broad-based movement "academic eclecticism," referring both to the scholarly grasp of antecedents and their subtle blending. By the 1880s, leading firms like McKim, Mead & White, in New York, and Henry Hobson Richardson, in Boston, had set the stage for a sophisticated, historicist eclecticism that would characterize much of American architecture and urban planning through the mid-twentieth century.[2]

In California—more precisely, in the San Francisco Bay Area—the movement was launched in the 1890s by a group of architects recently arrived from the East Coast, including A. Page Brown, Bernard Maybeck, Willis Polk, and A. C. Schweinfurth, and by the English expatriate Ernest Coxhead. These men tapped into a rapidly expanding reservoir of wealthy, educated, and culturally ambitious clients who yearned to shed the rawness and vulgarity of what was still a pioneer society for the trappings of culture and sophistication. Architecture served as the perfect vehicle for this arriviste mentality: it could reshape the environment to provide the settings and symbols for a metropolitan drama of aspiration and reinvention at the farthest edge of a newly conquered continent. Architecture possessed the power to create the illusion of a past that never was, a history that never happened: it could graft this orphaned outpost of empire into the lineage of Athens and Rome, of Paris and London, of Spain and Mexico—indeed, of any time or place that could be imagined. Myth was central to the enterprise. The imagined past was a romantic ideal—as, for later generations, the imagined future would be. California, most mythic and exotic of American places, was resonant with images of enchantment and wealth. The state's Spanish-Mexican heritage had given rise to fantasies of a pastoral Eden; its natural beauty engendered more durable dreams of an actual Eden, where the land retained the power to heal. Residential designers in the Arts and Crafts tradition contributed to this vision by manipulating materials, forms, space, and site in ways to suggest a timeless connection with nature. The symbolic heart of the Arts and Crafts house, for example, is the fireplace/chimney, a masonry shaft anchoring the structure to the earth and enshrining elemental heat and light in its cave-like hearth. As much as the refinements of Europe, these archaic impulses fed the stream of California architecture at the turn of the twentieth century.

More than any other Bay Area architect of his generation, Bernard Maybeck synthesized the diverse tendencies of the period. Donning the mantle of master illusionist in Berkeley, his adopted home, this graduate of the Ecole was able to create buildings within a broad band of allusive emotion, from the neverland medievalism of his Arts and Crafts residences to the poetic classicism of his public buildings. His shingled houses set the standard (and the stage) for the bohemian enclaves that took hold on the hillsides around the campus. He also initiated the study of architecture at the university, and under the patronage of Phoebe Apperson Hearst he oversaw the international competition for a new campus plan.

John Galen Howard, another alumnus of the Ecole des Beaux-Arts, came to Berkeley in 1902 as the supervising architect for the first-place plan and formally established the university's School of Architecture in 1903. By then, more than a dozen architects who had studied at the Ecole had set up practices in the Bay Area, including the first woman to attend the academy, Julia Morgan. So impeccable, and prolific, were her forays into academic eclecticism—most famously at San Simeon, the pleasure palace of William Randolph Hearst (Phoebe's famous son)—that her name became associated in the popular mind with just about any well-designed building in historical dress. Yet she was merely one of the best and the brightest of a whole generation of eclectic architects that flourished in the Bay Area in the first half of the twentieth century.

WALTER HARRIS RATCLIFF was born in England on February 2, 1881, in Blackheath, Kent, the London suburb where his father, Walter Henry Ratcliff, served as headmaster of a boys' school. His grandfather, Joseph Ratcliff (1808–1864), was the fifth of eight children born to a family that had become prominent in brass manufacturing in Birmingham, the industrial center of the English Midlands, famed for metal processing. Joseph was the third oldest of six sons. His older brother Sir John Ratcliff served a term as mayor of Birmingham; another brother, Thomas, became an Anglican minister.[3]

Joseph managed the family firm, Ratcliff & Son, and in partnership with his brother Edmund established the Birmingham foundry of J & E Ratcliff. Among the best-known brass products associated with the Ratcliff name were railroad-car lamps, carriage harness plates, candlesticks, letter clips, and postal scales, or letter weights, introduced after the inauguration of the "penny post" in 1839 (when postage began to be charged by weight rather than distance). The company, which evolved into the Ratcliff Brass Works, prospered over the years from the sale of gas fittings, automobile parts, shell casings, and other products essential to a modern industrial society. It grew to include several foundries by the early twentieth century.

In 1832, around the time J & E Ratcliff was established, Joseph Ratcliff married Mary Ann Rowlinson, whose father also owned a brass foundry. They had eight children, a daughter and seven sons, born between 1834 and 1849. The oldest son, Howard Taylor Ratcliff (1836–1909), eventually took over the company. Walter Henry Ratcliff (1840–1925) was the third oldest son, as his father had been.

Despite his family's heritage—its earthy immersion in an industrial realm—Walter entered the more abstract world of theology, which he studied at Cambridge; like his Uncle Thomas, he became an Anglican minister. Was this path taken by choice or by necessity? As a younger son, he may have been excluded from a role in the family

The Reverend Walter Henry Ratcliff.

business; as an intellectual, he may have fled from it. If so, he would likely have been drawn to the anti-industrial tenets of the English Arts and Crafts movement and the associated aesthetic of the High Church Gothic Revival. By all accounts he was a bookish man who chose teaching over a pastoral ministry. Yet it seems he did not need to work; an annual income of six hundred pounds from the family freed him from such practicalities.[4]

Walter gravitated to London, where he could sate his cerebral appetites at the museums, libraries, and lecture halls of an imperial capital of several million residents. It was there, in the summer of 1878, that Ratcliff, 38, married the 24-year-old Evelyn Anne Harris at St. Luke's Church on Redcliffe Square.[5] In six years they had three children, all born in or near London. The two daughters, Evelyn Marianne (Mary) and Ethel Bridget, were born in 1879 and 1883, bracketing the arrival of the middle child and only son, Walter Harris, in 1881.

For reasons that are unclear but seem to have been related to the parents' health, the family eventually left England for America. They sailed out of Southampton on the steamship *Paris,* arriving at Ellis Island, in New York Harbor, on June 2, 1894. Their destination was California, and their protracted odyssey, which began with a trip across the continent by train, passed though San Diego and Pasadena before ending in Berkeley in 1897. Each stage of this northward pilgrimage in California suggested a search for some ideal combination of culture and climate: from the raw commercialism of San Diego to the more literate parlors of Pasadena, and finally to Berkeley, where ideas flowed as freely as the sparkling bayside breezes.

THOUGH still a small town at the turn of the twentieth century, with a population under fifteen thousand, Berkeley was a cultural center—home to a diverse community of scholars, writers, and artists, an incubator of experimental lifestyles and innovative architecture. The intellectual heart of the town—indeed, its raison d'etre—was the University of California; the campus, on a grassy upland at the foot of the East Bay hills, opened in 1873, five years after the university was founded. The town itself was incorporated in 1878, including within its boundaries a bayshore settlement called Ocean View.

As recalled by his grandson Robert, Walter Henry Ratcliff's decision to settle in Berkeley was strongly influenced by the presence of the university: "My grandfather was not a great moneymaker, but he was very concerned about education . . . They came to Berkeley so that the three children could go to the university."[6] The Ratcliffs were cosmopolitan travelers, accustomed to life in a great world city whose population exceeded that of the entire state of California. How quaint, how charming Berkeley must have seemed to them, its smallness accentuated by the expansive beauty of its setting.

They took up residence in a rented house in the Northside, an upland enclave north of campus favored by professors, professionals, and free-thinkers of various stripes. It was also an early center of the California Arts and Crafts movement, and its sensibilities would have felt familiar to the English family. Local proponents such as the writer and naturalist Charles Keeler persuaded Northside residents to form the Hillside Club, in 1898, as a means of promoting and protecting the natural setting and rustic architecture. In 1904, Keeler would also publish *The Simple Home,* a classic primer on Arts and Crafts design, decoration, and gardening.[7] The neighborhood quickly became celebrated for its shingled redwood houses clinging to oak-studded slopes overlooking the bay.

In 1902, Walter and Evelyn Ratcliff moved into their own shingled house at the northeast corner

Berkeley still had a bucolic feeling in the late nineteenth century. This 1890s view takes in the campus and hills from the vicinity of Shattuck Avenue.

of Euclid Avenue and Virginia Street, a central Northside location three blocks from campus. Robert remembered the residence as a reflection of its milieu: "It was a two-story house, with four bedrooms . . . an old Berkeley Craftsman-type house [with] wooden shingles."[8] Robert also retained vivid memories of his grandfather:

> [He] spent his entire time reading. . . . He used to sit in his study, with his feet up on his desk, and smoke a pipe. He had sulfur matches, made from a block of wood [that] had been put in a press . . . and he would be constantly lighting his pipe. The combination of the smell of these sulfur matches and the smoke was something else. I just remember his sitting there in a cloud of smoke.

As the Ratcliffs immersed themselves in the community—teas and soirees, lectures and concerts, tennis and hiking, Hillside Club and Sierra Club—Walter Sr. joined the ranks of Berkeley's bearded sages. The erudite clergyman with his Cambridge degree and refined accent fit seamlessly into the loose-knit circles of the town's intellectual elite. Over six feet tall, with a white beard set off by the dome of his balding head, he cut an impressive figure striding up and down hills and across campus. Though he did not have a full-time congregation—he was not so compelled—he would officiate upon request, in High Church regalia of robe and staff, uttering the sacred rites in mellifluous Latin.[9]

THE SPIRITUAL tenor of Berkeley resonated with the Reverend Ratcliff, and he participated in the serious business of molding that mindset and endowing it with theological legitimacy. A liberal Christian, open to modern currents of thought in art, science, philosophy, and political theory, he found in Berkeley a like-minded community of clergymen and biblical scholars, particularly at the Pacific Theological Seminary. Established in 1866 by the Congregational Church, which had also played a role in starting the University of

California, the seminary was the oldest graduate school of religion west of the Mississippi.[10]

The inclusive, optimistic Christianity enshrined at Berkeley at the dawn of the twentieth century underlay the intoxicating humanism of the age. Modern churchmen, influenced by Darwin, Hegel, and Marx, espoused a gospel of human perfectibility. The New Jerusalem—the ordained end of history, the long-sought society of perfect love and justice—would not be handed down from on high; it would be designed and built on earth. On tiptoe, gazing out to the infinite blue horizon beyond the Golden Gate, how sure the dreamers and doers of Berkeley must have been of its arrival. How well this brand of millenarian utopianism suited—and explained—their lifestyle.

And if men and women could work together to create a perfect world, in harmony with the divine course of history, they had the intricate beauties of divine creation to sustain them. Awesome and serene, solemn and joyful, nature could bring the beholder into contact with the immanent mind of God. But this required vision. The good citizens of Berkeley were fortunate in this regard, for they had a seer nearby in the person of John Muir. Equal parts mystic and scientist, poet and prophet, Scottish-born Muir had arrived in California in the 1860s, finding in the Sierra Nevada a prooftext of his theology of the redemptive role of nature. Like all great preaching, his words inspired and instructed, as in this passage from a letter written in Yosemite in 1870:

> I have not been to church a single time since leaving home. Yet this glorious valley might be called a church, for every lover of the great Creator who

comes within the broad overwhelming influences of the place fails not to worship as he never did before. The glory of the Lord is upon all his works; it is written plainly upon all the fields of every clime, and upon every sky, but here in this place of surpassing glory the Lord has written in capitals.[11]

The Sierra Club, founded in San Francisco in 1892 with Muir as its first president, had many Berkeley members, the Ratcliffs among them. When the club initiated its annual "High Trip" to the Sierra, in 1901, Mary, Ethel, and young Walter were frequent participants, and through the club they met such luminaries as William Colby, William Frederic Badè, Marion Randall Parsons, and Muir himself. Badè, a protégé of Muir who became his biographer and literary executor, moved to Berkeley in 1902 to fill the chair of professor of Old Testament literature and Semitic languages at the Pacific Theological Seminary. Among his works, *The Old Testament in the Light of Today* and *The Life and Letters of John Muir* are classics of their genres.

In 1906, when he was 36, Badè married the 27-year-old Mary Ratcliff, whom he had met on a Sierra Club outing. The wedding took place at St. Mark's Church, the pioneer Episcopalian congregation in Berkeley; her father officiated, assisted by the president of the seminary. Mary died the following year giving birth to their first child.[12] Badè remained close to the family; Muir, a warm acquaintance.

Ethel's marriage early in 1911 seemed almost to reprise her sister's: she was 27; the groom was 36; the wedding was held at St. Mark's. The difference was that Ethel married her first cousin, Martin

Rowlinson Ratcliff, the youngest son of her Uncle Howard, who had courted her during her yearlong trip to Europe and the British Isles the previous year. The couple moved back to England, where Martin carried on his father's business and Ethel became a star on the amateur tennis circuit.[13] His two sisters gone, it fell to the brother to carry on the family legacy in California.

THE TRAJECTORY of the son's life was unlike his father's. In his education and career, Walter Harris Ratcliff gravitated to the tangibility of things rather than the abstraction of ideas—the physical world of matter to be studied, of materials to be felt and fashioned into something new. He seemed to look back to England, to the foundries of Birmingham, as if to forge a bond with his industrial heritage. One sensed the influence again of his father's older brother Howard, the proverbial rich uncle who became his nephew's patron.

Yet in his embrace of the natural world Walter followed in his father's footsteps, whether he knew it or not. The theological burden of the father became in the son a tacit belief, one shared by many in Berkeley's enchanted groves. Call it the deconstruction of heaven or the divinization of earth, it amounted to the same thing: the adoration of nature and exaltation of community—the worship of life itself. Muir and Maybeck framed this worldview, the one providing its most poetic theological rationale, the other its most potent settings and symbols. In them the Arts and Crafts ethos was confirmed. Young Ratcliff knew both men, and his life attested to his ingrained sense of being in the world. Joined to his love of art and

nature was a grounded, pragmatic temperament that placed a high value on craftsmanship, competence, economy, and work.

He loved the smell of plaster, the feel of lumber, the heft of a tool; he loved to work with his hands. "I don't know that they had a screwdriver or a hammer in their house when he was growing up," his son Robert recalled. "When he built his house he built himself a workshop, a great big workshop." It occupied a place of honor in the family home, next to the dining room, screened by an arcade on the terrace. "He always had something he wanted to do, and that went on just about to the end of his life. If he'd go to the country, he was always fixing something, or building." The importance of work, of productive activity, would remain a defining family trait.

Walter's first few years in high school were spent in Pasadena, at the Throop Polytechnic Institute—later to become the California Institute of Technology (Caltech)—where he was able to choose from a wide range of technical and vocational subjects. Following his graduation from Berkeley High School, in 1898—according to the school yearbook, his ambition was "a home in England"; his destiny, "English lord"; his chief attainment, "champion tennis player"; his failing, "cheek"—he enrolled in the University of California, with a major in chemistry. He excelled in the field, serving as an assistant to the department chairman and receiving an academic award for experiments. He had to give up chemistry for his health, however: confined laboratory work apparently caused problems with his eyesight and teeth.[14]

Ratcliff's interest in architecture began during his undergraduate years at the University of California—not through formal training, though he may have taken courses in drawing, but by the less probable path of designing houses as a business venture.[15] His parents seem to have provided the initial impetus for these youthful forays into design, handing their son his first job when he was a student. In a contract notice from the summer of 1901—the earliest known record of a building designed by him—his mother is shown as the owner of a "frame dwelling" to be built in Berkeley's Southside; this was an investment property, built on speculation (intended for resale or rental). A second contract, from 1902, again with his mother listed as owner, was for the Ratcliff family residence in the Northside. In both contracts, young Ratcliff is listed as "architect."[16]

Another patron and associate in these early enterprises was his friend Charles Louis McFarland. Ten years older than Ratcliff, McFarland was born and raised in Washington, D.C., where his father worked as a patent attorney. The family moved to California in the late 1890s, residing in San Diego and Santa Barbara before settling in Berkeley in 1907. An only child who lived with his parents and never married, McFarland became an investor and financier in partnership with his father. How Ratcliff met him is not known, but as early as 1901, the 20-year-old student designed a speculative house for him, inaugurating a lifelong professional relationship.[17]

When Ratcliff graduated from the University of California in 1903 at age 22, he had already abandoned chemistry as a career and tried his hand at

Student portrait of Walter H. Ratcliff, Jr.

designing houses. The shift from chemistry to architecture could be seen as a shift in scale rather than kind—from the structure of matter at a microscopic scale to structural materials on a human scale—with both disciplines demanding of their devotees a profound engagement with the physical world. At any rate, the design experience must have had a galvanizing effect on him, for it marked the beginning of a new vocation.

THE YOUNG university graduate was perfectly placed in time and locale to feel the full force of the new architectural currents. For an aspiring architect at the turn of the twentieth century, few

House on Parker Street, Berkeley, 1901. This is Walter Ratcliff's earliest known work, designed for his parents when he was a university student; the shingle veneer may be a later addition.

the possibilities of an architecture rooted in the past yet highly original in conception. Hearst Hall (1899), a sort of throne-room for Phoebe Hearst, was a soaring Gothic fantasy, its great vaulted space spanned by cyclopean arches of laminated redwood. The more sedate Men's Faculty Club (1902) had an arcaded exterior of light-colored stucco, vaguely Roman and rational, encasing a darkly moody medieval interior. And there was the marvelous group of houses erected between 1895 and 1899 at Ridge Road and Highland Place, not far from the Ratcliff residence. The formal freedom, structural expressionism, and subtle historicism of these buildings represented the new eclecticism at its most brilliant, combining the allusive power of Old World imagery with the inventive élan of the New. They transcended style, offering glimpses of something timeless.

Maybeck's weren't the only notable buildings young Ratcliff would have seen during his formative years in Berkeley. There were works by Ernest Coxhead, Willis Polk, A. C. Schweinfurth, and other masters; buildings by any number of other competent architects; and, not least, a densely textured backdrop of development by a legion of often anonymous designers and builders, most evident in the hundreds of houses springing up every year in the cities and towns of the East Bay. Across the bay was San Francisco itself, easily accessible by train and ferry, where skyscrapers were being built with the most current

places could match Berkeley for the sheer excitement of its emerging scene, largely under the direction of Bernard Maybeck.[18] After a gestation that began in Paris in the 1880s and persisted through his early years in California, Maybeck had at last embarked on his independent career. In 1895, when he was 33, buildings began to stream forth as from a well of creative energy too long capped. At the same time, he orchestrated Phoebe Apperson Hearst's well-funded international competition for a new master plan for the Berkeley campus, drawing the attention of architects from around the world.

During Ratcliff's student years, Maybeck designed buildings in Berkeley that demonstrated

Hearst Hall, 1899. Bernard Maybeck, architect. Moved to the campus in 1901 from its original Southside location on Channing Way, the building burned in 1922.

technologies, the most advanced mechanical systems, and the most modern materials. For Ratcliff, intent on learning his new discipline, the region was like an architectural laboratory where experiments occurred daily.

WALTER RATCLIFF's fledgling career included three years of employment and apprenticeship in the office of John Galen Howard, from 1903 to 1906; a year abroad, studying and traveling, in 1906 and 1907; a short-lived partnership with Alfred Henry Jacobs, in 1907 and 1908; and the start of his independent practice in Berkeley late in 1908.[19]

In all of this, he was largely self-taught. Except for half a year or less at the British School in Rome, which then had no formal architectural course, his knowledge accrued from his observation of the work of other architects, his employment in Howard's office, his time abroad, and extensive reading. His timing was excellent. The profession was still porous enough to accept many practitioners without formal training—Ratcliff would receive his license to practice in 1906—and the economy was on the cusp of sustained growth after the recessionary 1890s.

In his employment with John Galen Howard, which served as an apprenticeship, Ratcliff could not have found a more qualified mentor. Howard personified the architectural elite in the United States. A native of New England, he had studied at

Downtown Berkeley, looking north on Shattuck Avenue from Allston Way, 1905. Ratcliff would open his office in the five-story First National Bank Building (just right of center) several years later.

the Massachusetts Institute of Technology, home to the oldest school of architecture in America, and later enrolled, and excelled, at the Ecole des Beaux-Arts. He had worked in two of the country's most prominent offices, Henry Hobson Richardson and McKim, Mead & White, and had established his own partnership in New York.

In 1898, Howard placed fourth out of 105 entries in the International Competition for the Phoebe A. Hearst Architectural Plan for the University of California. The winner, a Parisian named Emile Bénard, produced a Beaux-Arts plan with grand buildings oriented around a sloping axis that cut through the center of the campus. But Bénard was not retained by the Regents to supervise construction. The man hired for this

James T. Allen house, Mosswood Road, Berkeley, 1911. This Panoramic Hill residence of a professor of classics at the university typified Ratcliff's later work in the Arts and Crafts mode.

Hearst Memorial Mining Building, University of California, Berkeley. John Galen Howard, architect. This postcard view shows the building several years after its completion in 1907.

job was Howard. In 1902 he moved to Berkeley, where he would remain for over 25 years, leaving an indelible imprint on the campus and community.[20]

John Galen Howard came to Berkeley not only to oversee implementation of Bénard's plan but also to begin construction of a major campus building for Phoebe Apperson Hearst. Intended as a monument to her late husband, who made his fortune in mining, the Hearst Memorial Mining Building was four years under construction (1903 to 1907) and cost in excess of $1 million, an enormous sum for the time. It housed the world's largest college of mining and, in its planning, mechanical systems, materials, and overall design, was a major American building of its period—one of masterworks of the Berkeley campus.

The astronomical budget of the Mining Building, along with other, mostly campus-related projects, allowed Howard to hire a large staff. His office was run like an atelier at the Ecole des Beaux-Arts, serving as a training ground and springboard for architects who went on to long and productive careers in the Bay Area, most famously Julia Morgan and John Hudson Thomas. One member of the office staff from those years recalled:

> Each morning around 10:30 Mr. Howard, accompanied by his office superintendent, and sometimes by his engineer, would make the rounds of the tables, observing the progress of the work, discussing details or making comments . . . He was exceedingly pleasant spoken and gave you the impression of being very sincere and wholly interested in you as a person and in whatever you happened to be talking about . . . [He] seemed at all times to have complete mastery of any situation, knew exactly what he wanted to accomplish, and was quite ready to accept the views of others. No one had any hesitation in offering their opinion, and he received it and considered it for what it could be worth.[21]

To work in an office of this caliber presented the opportunity of a lifetime. Ratcliff went to work for Howard in 1903, soon after graduating from the university—the same year, ironically, that Howard began teaching architecture there.[22] The experience brought him into collegial contact with highly skilled architects and exposed him to challenges of design and construction at highly technical levels. This earnest, intelligent, and polished young man, serious about work and eager to learn, would likely have appealed to the equally serious older architect. Ratcliff was given greater responsibilities, including on-site monitoring of construction of the Hearst Memorial Mining Building.

By the time he left Howard's employ, in 1906, Ratcliff had been certified by the State Board of Architectural Examiners. He received his license in March of that year, shortly before earthquake and fire destroyed much of San Francisco (including Howard's downtown office). That fall, soon after his sister Mary's wedding, he set sail for England for a yearlong sabbatical of travel and study. He had left his homeland a 13-year-old boy; he returned a 25-year-old man—a licensed architect at the outset of his career.

WALTER RATCLIFF's year abroad served as a palpable introduction to the history of Western architecture, from the monuments of Italy and France to the vernacular cottages and churches of England, rekindling boyhood memories and instilling a sense of tradition that would sustain him through his career. The trip was underwritten by his Uncle Howard, head of the Ratcliff Brass Works, who also provided letters of introduction to well-placed friends on the Continent and helped secure his nephew's admission to the British School in Rome.

Ratcliff approached the sabbatical not as a vacation but as an opportunity to further his training and enhance his standing. The "grand tour" was a time-honored tradition, a rite of passage as important in its way as obtaining a license. He had no time to waste. At the outset of the twentieth century, architecture was a rapidly expanding profession with many formally trained practitioners who carried the cachet of a degree from an American or European school—not least the new school of architecture at the University of California. If he wished to compete at the highest levels of his profession, Ratcliff needed the imprimatur of travel and study in Europe.

The British School in Rome, where he studied for six months or so, had been established in 1901 as a government-sponsored research center modeled after the Roman academies of France, Germany, Austria, and other nations. Such schools made it possible for students of various nationalities to immerse themselves in the art, architecture, literature, and language of one of the world's cultural capitals. The British School attracted a wide range of scholars, including artists from the

Ratcliff (second from right, standing) with other members of John Galen Howard's office staff.

Royal Academy and members of the Royal Institute of British Architects. When Ratcliff attended the school, there was no formal course in architecture. A systematic survey of the city's buildings, however, would have exposed him to major monuments of the classical, Renaissance, and Baroque eras.[23]

Ratcliff headed on to France in the spring of 1907. In Paris he may have enrolled in one of the many architectural studios or drawing schools that catered to foreign students. Paris was then at the height of its influence as a center for architectural education, and the city prospered from a steady flow of aspirants; more Americans than ever were attending the Ecole des Beaux-Arts. World War I and the rise of modernism would soon bring an end to the preeminence of the Ecole, but few in Paris that spring could have conceived of such a future. In April Ratcliff traveled around France drawing buildings. His sketches from the expedition, which included visits to Tours and the chateaus of the Loire Valley, attested to his acquired skills. He ended his trip back in England, and in July sailed from Southampton to New York on the ocean liner *Teutonic*.

Ratcliff returned home in time for the August 23 dedication of the Hearst Memorial Mining Building. Embedded in one of the foundations was a gold watch, a gift from his Uncle Howard that had fallen from his vest as he observed concrete being poured into a form: the loss had pained him considerably. But time had passed; he had moved on; like the new campus building, his apprenticeship was complete.

Ratcliff produced this watercolor and garden plan of the Villa d'Este, Tivoli, in 1907 while attending the British School in Rome.

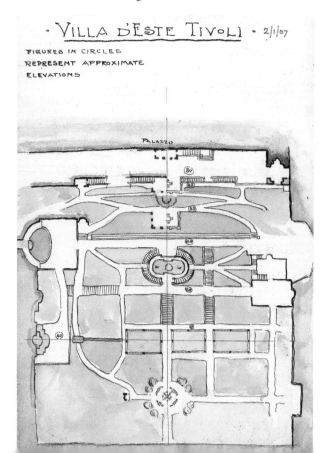

Ratcliff's travel sketches in France in the spring of 1907. Three depict chateaus in the Loire Valley; one is a scene in Tours.

Two Getting Established

IN THE summer of 1907, as Walter Harris Ratcliff made the long passage home by transatlantic ship and transcontinental train, a construction boom of unprecedented scale was entering its second year in the Bay Area. In the fifteen months since April 1906, when earthquake and fire had gutted the heart of San Francisco, six thousand buildings had been completed and another three thousand were under construction there. From the East Bay, the city's skyline seemed perpetually hazed by skeins of steel as new buildings rose from the ashes of the old. San Francisco's recovery would be celebrated at the 1915 Panama-Pacific International Exposition, an ephemeral Beaux-Arts spectacle in the spirit of the 1893 Chicago Columbian Exposition, and it would be enshrined in the City Beautiful ensemble of the civic center.[1]

Yet it was not in San Francisco alone that the aftereffects of the catastrophe were felt. Though the earthquake caused relatively little damage outside the city, it resulted in a substantial migration of businesses and residents to the East Bay suburbs of Berkeley, Oakland, and Alameda. At the same time, people streamed into the region from elsewhere. In 1900, the combined populations of Oakland, Berkeley, and Alameda remained under one hundred thousand; by 1910, they topped two hundred thousand; at the end of World War I they neared three hundred thousand.

The advent of the Key Route, in 1903, and the Southern Pacific's new interurban service, in 1911, gave the East Bay a superb system of electric streetcars and trains linked to ferries that made frequent crossings to San Francisco.[2] As the Key Route and Southern Pacific extended their lines through Berkeley's flatlands and into the hills, entire districts of farmland and scenic upland were opened to development. The town became a small

Walter H. Ratcliff house, Roble Road, Berkeley, 1914.

city, its population increasing from less than fifteen thousand in 1900 to over forty thousand in 1910, approaching sixty thousand by 1920.[3] Berkeley remained a center of architectural achievement. By World War I, the university had become the second largest in the nation, with seven thousand students; and under the guidance of John Galen Howard the campus had begun to assume the appearance of an idealized city of learning, its granite-clad monuments rising in tandem with the gleaming new city of commerce across the bay. In its orderly plan and in buildings like the Doe Memorial Library, Wheeler Hall, and Sather Tower—the splendid Campanile that announced Berkeley to the world—the Beaux-Arts campus infused a modern American university with the gravitas of history.

Beyond the campus, in its commercial districts and residential neighborhoods, Berkeley was equally transformed. Adjoined by the 1909 Beaux-Arts City Hall—the beginning of Berkeley's own City Beautiful civic center—the downtown along Shattuck Avenue acquired a collection of substantial masonry buildings, second only to Oakland in the East Bay as an urban center. Commercial enclaves expanded near the campus, notably along Telegraph Avenue, and others took hold in new residential tracts to the north and south.

The subdivisions were laid out in relation to the streetcar and train routes by huge real estate firms like the Realty Syndicate (a corporate cousin of the Key Route) and by local concerns such as Mason-McDuffie. New houses spread across the flatlands in a checkerboard of blocks and lots that lapped against hillsides, where the tracts morphed into the winding streets of Claremont, Northbrae, Cragmont, and Thousand Oaks. In the vicinity of the campus, remaining parcels in the older tracts of the Northside and Southside rapidly filled.

This was the milieu of an expanding coterie of architects, among them graduates of the university's new school of architecture, who would carry on the distinguished local tradition of residential design begun in the 1890s by Maybeck, Coxhead, Schweinfurth, and others. Now in his forties, Maybeck had dozens of houses to his credit, many of them overlooking the campus he had helped bring into being. The new generation active in Berkeley, including Julia Morgan, John Hudson Thomas, Louis Christian Mullgardt, Albert Farr, and William C. Hays, would soon be joined by Walter H. Ratcliff, Jr.

WITHIN weeks of his return, Ratcliff entered into a partnership with the architect Alfred Henry Jacobs. A fellow alumnus of the class of 1903 at the University of California, Jacobs had pursued his formal training at the Massachusetts Institute of Technology, where he graduated in 1905, followed by a year of study at the Ecole des Beaux-Arts. He received his license to practice in California in June 1906, three months after Ratcliff. The death of his father, a prominent San Francisco businessman, in June 1907 gave him the means to start his own practice.

The firm, known as Ratcliff & Jacobs, maintained its office in San Francisco, where Jacobs

Bedroom addition to the Ratcliff house, 1923. The big window slides down, to open up the room to the patio.

resided.[4] It produced little during its brief existence, which lasted a little over a year. Its few documented commissions included two small apartment buildings and two houses in San Francisco; a pair of speculative houses in Piedmont; and two houses in Berkeley. Its best-known building in the East Bay was a shingled clubhouse for the Berkeley Tennis Club, erected in the Southside in the spring of 1908—a job that would have come into the office through Ratcliff's extensive tennis contacts.[5] The partnership did not endure, for various reasons. The family memory is that the partners did not get along, and that Ratcliff did not enjoy commuting to San Francisco; he wanted to be independent, and he wanted to be in Berkeley. The *Daily Pacific Builder* announced the firm's dissolution on December 4, 1908.[6]

By then, Walter H. Ratcliff, Jr., Architect, age 27, had opened for business on the second floor of the First National Bank Building in downtown Berkeley. The five-story tower, erected in 1903, was one of the city's tallest commercial buildings, and arguably its handsomest—suavely designed by John Galen Howard with an arcaded base and crisp rows of windows on unadorned brick facades.[7] Like the Ratcliff & Jacobs office in San Francisco, this was a surprisingly desirable business address for a start-up. Ratcliff knew the building well, having worked there in 1904 and 1905, when Howard's office was on the top floor. In his first twelve months in Room 211—destined to be his office for the next ten years—he would receive twice as many commissions as in his fifteen months with Jacobs.

Ratcliff's decision to establish a practice in Berkeley clearly made sound economic sense, revealing the sort of business acumen that led him to design houses in the first place. The city's red-hot real estate market, fueled primarily by residential construction, presented an unparalleled opportunity for the young architect. His social and academic standing within the community provided an entrée; his ambition and drive produced the result—in less than five years, a well-known practice marked by critical and commercial success. The move from San Francisco, locus of the profession, to suburban Berkeley had not been without risk, but the gamble paid off.

Through World War I, the large majority of Walter Ratcliff's work would remain in Berkeley, and most of these jobs would be residential in nature. Approximately 150 commissions bearing his name have been documented between 1901 and 1916. Around two dozen of these jobs dated from his years as a student, apprentice, and partner with Jacobs; the rest came out of his office. Nearly 120 of the commissions—80 percent—were for houses. Berkeley jobs likewise accounted for 80 percent of the architect's total output, including three-fourths of his houses. Walter Ratcliff's peak period of residential work, from 1909 to 1912, coincided with the start of his independent practice, and he designed at least eighty houses in those four years—twenty sets of plans on average per annum, over a third of which were commissioned by investors (including himself) who built houses on speculation, i.e., for resale or rental.[8]

Ratcliff owed much of his early success in Berkeley to the patronage of Duncan McDuffie, a college friend and fellow outdoorsman who was best man at his sister Mary's wedding. Four years his senior, McDuffie had, since his graduation from the University of California in 1899, become the city's best-known residential developer. An active partner in numerous real estate companies, notably Mason-McDuffie, he helped lay the foundation for Berkeley's post-earthquake growth in sprawling patchwork developments like Claremont and Northbrae, stitched together between 1905 and 1910 from fifteen separate tracts.

McDuffie was the quintessential Berkeley developer. A lifelong member (and twice president) of the Sierra Club, he imbued his subdivisions with a picturesque, natural romanticism inspired by the example of Frederick Law Olmsted—curving streets that followed the contours of the hills, sequestered paths and stairways, rustic stone retaining walls and entrance pylons, and plantings of trees and flowers. His deeds often included restrictions for minimum setbacks and construction costs. He cultivated like-minded architects, either hiring them outright—as in the case of John Galen Howard, who designed pylons and other streetscape features in Claremont and Northbrae—or passing them on to prospective clients who purchased land. Walter Ratcliff, Henry Gutterson, and John Hudson Thomas designed dozens of houses in Claremont and Northbrae, and in the latter development Ratcliff also assisted in design review. With their hillside settings, bay views, and high level of design, from layout and landscaping to individual houses, these subdivisions were among the most desirable in the East

Speculative house for Claremont Land Co., Tunnel Road, Berkeley, 1912. This was one of Ratcliff's early essays in English revivalism.

Bay, favored by businessmen, professionals, and academics.[9]

Of equal importance to Ratcliff's professional rise was the continued support of his parents and his longtime associate Charles Louis McFarland. In 1907, McFarland moved to Berkeley with his father and stepmother and soon became Ratcliff's principal client, providing the architect with a fifth of his residential commissions in his first three years of independent practice. Their business relationship was formalized toward the end of 1911 with the incorporation of Alameda County Home Builders, Inc., a real estate and development firm

in which McFarland and Ratcliff and their fathers served as the four coequal shareholders and directors. Described in the articles of incorporation as a "land and land improvement and building company," the firm was managed by the younger McFarland; its office was on the second floor of the First National Bank Building, down the hall from Ratcliff's architectural office.[10]

Ratcliff's Berkeley houses were situated for the most part in the new upland tracts; over half were in Claremont and Northbrae, and Claremont alone accounted for fully a fourth of the architect's residential output prior to World War I. Most of his remaining houses were built in Oakland, with a scattering of isolated commissions in and around the Bay Area, including Piedmont, Concord, Belvedere, San Francisco, Palo Alto, and Santa Cruz.

A COMPARISON of Walter Ratcliff's earliest residential designs with the later ones in this period reveals how diligently he applied himself to the task of becoming an architect in a milieu where architecture was judged by the highest standards. His more nuanced work was done for clients who intended to live in their houses—who typically had bigger budgets at their disposal and a deeper personal interest in the outcome. They included professors, publishers, engineers, attorneys, doctors, dentists, realtors, financiers, and managers in mining, construction, lumber, and produce. Houses designed for investors, who commissioned them with an eye to profit, were generally less

Living room, house on Tunnel Road. The beams of the high ceiling meet the mullion posts of the south-facing bay window.

Herbert G. Zuckerman house, Mendocino Avenue, Berkeley, 1911: a picturesque Northbrae residence exhibiting the architect's transition, prior to World War I, from a rustic idiom to a more understated stucco palette.

expensive to build and more standardized in massing, styling, and plan.[11]

In most projects, regardless of client or budget, Ratcliff tended toward balanced compositions and plans, preferring the Beaux-Arts rationalism of the American Renaissance to the more intuitive romanticism of American Arts and Crafts. In this he was not unusual; most architects and clients of his era seemed more comfortable with the conservatism of classical order than the vagaries of personal expression. Julia Morgan, whose Beaux-Arts approach to Arts and Crafts design produced an urbane rusticity permeated with symmetry and harmony, exemplified the prevailing tastes of the era.

Ratcliff's first designs, the products of a self-taught 20-year-old, resembled the myriad of houses turned out by contractors in the Bay Area at the turn of the twentieth century. The two speculative houses he produced in 1901 for his parents and McFarland were boxy, hip-roofed structures with Colonial Revival styling and standard central-hall or side-hall plans. Shingles soon replaced siding as finish on his exteriors, but the hip-roofed box with side- or central-hall plan persisted in his early work, as in the Southside house commissioned by the McFarland family in 1907.[12]

Later speculative designs tended toward two-story, gable-roofed forms with symmetrical façades and central-hall plans, regardless of stylistic treatment. Two houses in Claremont typified this trend. The first, built for his sister Ethel in 1908, was Arts and Crafts in feeling, with quaint dormers and a veneer of shingles. Though the second, commissioned by McFarland in 1911, had plain façades sheathed in stucco, both shared a general symmetry of form and plan.[13]

Walter Ratcliff's work for speculators included numerous bungalows. Since these small, inexpensive cottages were often built in groups of two or three or more, he gave them distinguishing touches—a chimney, a window, a type of shingling, a beamed ceiling—to convey a sense of individuality. On first glance, a row of three Oakland bungalows built in 1911 for McFarland was virtually indistinguishable from standard pattern-book

William Frederic Badè house, College Avenue, Berkeley, 1906. This shingled house was one of Ratcliff's early works in the Arts and Crafts mode.

versions produced by East Bay contractors; closer examination revealed the subtlety of the details.[14]

In his more elaborate houses for individual clients, Ratcliff clearly revealed his development as a designer in transition from amateur and apprentice to professional. His first such commission was the 1902 Ratcliff family residence. The $3,700 budget, double that of his previous jobs, resulted in a stretched-out, two-story box with a turret-like bay bulging from the front corner. Sheathed in shingles, the house had a whiff of Maybeck in its steep hip roof with diminutive dormers arrayed along the slopes. The design was conservative for its milieu, but not amateurish; it blended Colonial Revival massing with an Arts and Crafts palette

and a dash of medievalism to achieve a relaxed and roomy charm.

Two Southside houses dating from his employment with John Galen Howard revealed Walter Ratcliff's shift to the Arts and Crafts mode. The carefully composed rusticity of the 1904 Ernest Mead residence represented his first full essay in the idiom. A shingled box with broad gable roof, the house had picturesque elevations made up of corner bays, a clinker-brick chimney, banded lattice windows, and an offset gabled entry. A terrace-like porch ran across the front, open to sky and garden. Windows and entry were quaintly shrunk to make the house appear larger—a manipulation of scale, in the manner of Coxhead, that

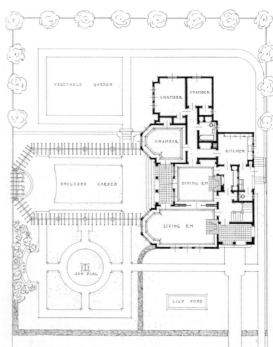

Anna Head house, Belrose Avenue, Berkeley, 1911, with first floor and garden plan. House and garden were integrally linked in the residence of the prominent educator who introduced Walter Ratcliff to his future wife.

would become a recurring strain in Ratcliff's work. The redwood interior had a conventional plan, reprising the standard side-hall configuration. The 1906 Badè residence commissioned by his sister and brother-in-law was less stiff in its massing, achieving a sense of ease in the balanced play of multiple gables, flaring eaves, window canopies, and sunroom balcony. The more or less symmetrical composition had a central-hall plan.[15]

By the time Ratcliff established his Berkeley practice, he was skilled at designing Arts and Crafts houses that fit quietly into their residential settings. Most, like the Badè residence, were

balanced compositions. Yet in other shingled houses of the period, such as a large speculative residence built for McFarland in 1909 in Claremont, or the Elmer Buckman residence of the same year in Northbrae, Ratcliff succeeded in creating picturesque buildings whose more relaxed massing and more open plans represented a stylistic advance over the box-like forms and standardized planning of earlier designs.[16]

WALTER RATCLIFF's residential work became increasingly overt in its historical references once he entered independent practice. In this, his development again paralleled that of Morgan and many other architects of his day. The tendency first manifested itself in faux half-timbering—stucco veneer inlaid with patterned wood—and pseudo-thatch shingle roofs with rounded edges and undulating eaves.[17] At the same time, interiors tended to be more ornate in their wood and plaster finishes, in contrast to the plainer paneling and plasterwork of his Arts and Crafts houses.

Whatever its origins—his boyhood, his family, his travels, most likely all three—a strong feeling for English antecedent emerged in the architect's work as early as the Badè house, conceived as an Arts and Crafts version of a Cotswold cottage, its quaint pseudo-thatch gables facing sideways to a garden. He reprised this scheme in his 1911 Claremont residence for Anna Head, an Arts and Crafts patron (and former congregant of his father's) who ran a well-known Berkeley girls' school.[18] With its rough-cast stucco veneer, high hip roof, and clustered casement windows, the house referenced English Arts and Crafts design, particularly that of Charles Voysey. The one-and-a-half-story cottage faced south to a garden laid out by Ratcliff with walkways and pergolas. Interior spaces were intimately linked to this garden: the dining room was set in the center of the house, opening onto a porch and adjoined by living room and bedroom wings with bay windows. In its stylish historicism, supple planning, and integration with the garden, this small house, designed when the architect was 30, represented a new level of synthesis.[19]

He was not in search of a single synthesis, however, and felt free to use whatever approach suited the client. In the years leading up to World War I, he acquired an eclectic palette that mixed

J. M. Howells house, Belvedere, 1911. Designed in 1910, this was one of Ratcliff's early residential designs with a stucco-and-tile palette. The Mission Revival mansion occupies a ridge-top site overlooking Sausalito and the Golden Gate.

Arthur H. Breed house, Piedmont, 1912; demolished. The arcaded loggia and balcony opened onto a rear courtyard.

Staircase and hall, Breed house.

his emergent English medievalism with Italian classicism, Spanish colonialism, and the contemporary influence of his peers. Though his imagery became less rustic, an Arts and Crafts sensibility persisted in the attention he gave to landscaping and to the integration of indoors and outdoors,

with the recurring use of the loggia, terrace, and balcony (often labeled "sleeping porch" or "deck" on his plans) as transitional elements. His stylistic breadth came from observation and immersion in his well-stocked library. "He actually had a librarian," Robert recalled. "The books were indexed and marked as they would be in a public library."

His academic classicism was put on display for the first time in the Piedmont mansion of the realtor and longtime state senator Arthur H. Breed, erected in 1912 in the newly fashionable upland enclave overlooking Oakland. At $30,000, it was by far the most opulent of Ratcliff's prewar houses. As if in homage to his mentor, the architect produced a textbook version of an Italian Renaissance palazzo that would not have felt out of place on Howard's campus. Set in landscaped grounds, the sprawling, H-plan residence had a symmetrical façade, with arcaded porches at the front and rear; walls were clad in stucco, the hip roof in terra-cotta tile. The plan stretched the entry into a perforated hyphen that ran the width of the house, flanked only by the loggias and views. This gallery-like hall, with a staircase at one end, linked the living room and library wing to a dining and service wing with kitchen and pantries as well as a breakfast room overlooking the rear garden. Servants' quarters were located on both levels of this wing. The upper floor contained six bedrooms and two "sleeping porches," one of them a long balcony over the rear loggia.[20]

Ratcliff's later essays employing a stucco-and-tile palette were less literal in their historical references. In these designs, he mixed Italian/Mediterranean classicism with elements of California Mission Revival—a synthesis he had first encountered, forcefully, in Howard's Hearst Memorial Mining Building. The Berkeley residence of publisher Thomas Shearman, built over the fall and winter of 1913 and 1914, occupied most of an irregular corner lot at the base of the hills near the campus. The plan responded creatively to the constricted site. Living room and library wings angled out from a lofty, six-sided stair hall adjoined by a dining/service/servant's wing extending to the rear. A wide porch led from the dining and breakfast rooms to a terrace garden that functioned as

an outdoor room, with exterior fireplace and a peristyle pergola around its four sides. Balconies and a belvedere served four upstairs bedrooms, and the interior featured lavish wood finish and four ornate fireplaces. The house's stucco veneer was delicately molded with classical motifs that contrasted with heavily carved wood elements under the tile-clad eaves.[21]

FOR HIS own residence, built in 1914, Ratcliff summed up his career to that point, combining a lightly classicized stucco-and-tile palette with Arts and Crafts massing to create a subtly eclectic design that felt at once old and new, traditional and up-to-date. He expunged any sense of "Englishness" from the exterior, as if to declare his independence from his own past and proclaim his self-made identity as husband, father, and architect.

Two years earlier, in June 1912, with Charles McFarland as best man, Walter Harris Ratcliff had entered into marriage with Muriel Cora Williams, the daughter of a prosperous businessman whose family arrived in San Francisco during the gold rush. Muriel was a graduate of the Anna Head School, and she ran in the same social circles as Walter. They shared a love of nature and tennis. Their courtship was kindled during visits to Bolinas, a picturesque hamlet in Marin County where both had friends; Walter proposed to her on the bay as they were crossing over to Marin.

Walter was 31 and Muriel was 20 when they wed. Their first child, Robert, arrived in May 1913. Muriel gave birth to a second son, Peter, in August 1914, on the day they began moving into their

Ernest A. Nickerson house, Tunnel Road, Berkeley, 1914.
This Claremont residence was the architect's last large
pre-World War I house.

newly completed residence at 55 Roble Road, perched in the hills above the Claremont Hotel.

Annexed to the city in 1906, the Claremont district remained largely undeveloped in the upland reaches east of Claremont Avenue, though Ratcliff had already designed nearly two dozen houses along the winding streets. The Ratcliffs' closest neighbor was Duncan McDuffie, whose stucco-and-tile residence (by John Galen Howard) was set in a ten-acre estate spreading across the slope below Roble Road. The Ratcliff residence revealed the influence of both Maybeck and Howard. Its massing, consisting of a gabled living room wing extending out from a two-story, cross-gabled section, echoed Maybeck's own residence in the hills north of campus.[22] The stucco-and-tile imagery owed more to Howard, as did the plan, which was modeled after Howard's first Northside

residence.[23] That house had an L-shaped plan, with a living room in the long axis and a dining room in the short axis served by a central hall entered from the west; the hall opened onto an east terrace enclosed by the wings.

Ratcliff utilized the same orientation and plan. One entered the house on a walkway bordering the west-facing front, through an arched porch. Steps led up from a foyer under the stair landing to a wood-paneled hall with glass doors looking out to the rear terrace. The living room, nearly thirty feet long, opened up to the right. This great room, with exposed trusses, dark wood paneling, and monumental fireplace, was the English heart of the house, intact within its California shell. The dining room, an intimate space with a fireplace and boxed beams, faced the terrace from the other side of the hall. Ratcliff's workshop lay beyond this room, screened from the terrace by a loggia. Stairs led up to two bedrooms and a study with yet another fireplace.[24]

Entry hall, Nickerson house. An eclectic Tudor/Renaissance flavor imbues the richly finished interior.

Down the street, at the corner of Tunnel Road, another house by Ratcliff neared completion as the architect and his family moved into their new home.[25] Commissioned by lumberman Ernest A. Nickerson, this large, eclectic residence was English with an Italian accent, blending medieval and classical idioms in a balanced composition of steep gables and arcaded loggia with odd mannerist columns. The plan reprised the spacious formality of the Breed mansion: a grand stair hall linking major rooms and opening onto a terrace overlooking the garden. A dining/servant's wing angled to one side; five bedrooms and two balcony/decks were on the upper floor. Finished in the fall of 1914, it was Ratcliff's last great house of the prewar years.

IF 1914 was a watershed year for Ratcliff in terms of residential work, it also marked his emergence as a versatile practitioner capable of handling an array of programmatic and technical problems. His office produced designs for fraternities, churches, parish halls, apartment buildings, clubs, fire stations, and schools. The larger of these buildings introduced the architect to structural systems and materials other than the wood framing, shingles, and stucco of his residential jobs, providing him with the opportunity to work with reinforced concrete, structural steel, brick curtain walls, and artificial stone (cast concrete) trim—not to mention mechanical systems like central heating and elevators.

In the midst of this expanding practice, Ratcliff drove himself to enter competitions, including designs for a school in Sacramento and for the new Alameda County Infirmary (now Fairmont Hospital) in San Leandro. His Beaux-Arts scheme for the hospital placed wards and other structures in an axial arrangement around a large administration building, on landscaped grounds, earning him a second-place prize in the competition.[26]

In all likelihood, though we have no firsthand accounts, Walter H. Ratcliff, Jr., emulated John Galen Howard in his business methods. Howard, after all, was the only architect he had observed at close hand over a period of time. Accordingly, Ratcliff would have cultivated the clients, managed the jobs, and directed the design process while overseeing and training the draftsmen who carried out his directives. As his practice grew, so did the size of his staff, and Ratcliff himself began to assume the mantle of mentor to a new generation of Bay Area architects.

How deep was his imprint on the designs that bore his name? We don't know, but given his work ethic, it was probably substantial. How many draftsmen did he employ? As the work increased in the years leading up to World War I, it is safe to assume that he had at least three or four assistants in his office at any one time. Robert Ratcliff, just out of architecture school in the 1930s, visited a number of offices looking for work; most of the architects, he recalled, told him that they had worked for his father at one time or another. Charles F. Masten, Lester W. Hurd, and William Raymond Yelland were among them.[27]

His father's contacts within the Episcopal diocese brought Ratcliff jobs for parish halls in San Francisco and Oakland as well as a small church in Oakland. The Mission of the Good Samaritan—his first ecclesiastical commission—was dedicated on Easter Sunday, 1910. The building's diminutive scale reflected its missionary function as an "outreach" facility; its shingled Arts and Crafts styling suited the residential setting; and the Tudor-Gothic trusses of the sanctuary spoke to the Anglican origins of the denomination. The 1914 parish hall for St. Peter's Church, in Oakland's Rockridge district, was also given Tudor styling.[28]

Ratcliff's prewar apartment buildings were among the architect's most visually prominent and technically advanced commissions. He designed as many as ten, most within walking distance of the Berkeley campus. Ranging in size from two to five stories, with four or more units, they were well-planned facilities, with varied apartment configurations and often with homelike amenities like fireplaces and sleeping porches. The three-story, fifteen-unit Glen Garry (1912) in the Northside, the architect's first large apartment building, was robustly sculpted with massive chimneys and balconies that contrasted with the cavernous voids of porches.[29] The similarly scaled Channing Apartments (1913) presented a calmer, classicized face to the street, with elements taken directly from the Hearst Memorial Mining Building. Wide bay windows flanked a monumental arch with architrave, and the broad sweep of the tiled roof ended in overhangs with heavy wood brackets.[30]

The five-story Cambridge Hotel Apartments (1914) rose from the campus commercial district on Telegraph Avenue. One of Berkeley's taller prewar buildings, it housed forty-eight apartments and four street-level storefronts. In its structural and mechanical complexity, the $80,000 project posed numerous technical challenges, providing the architect with his first exposure to steel framing, brick curtain walls, and elevator systems; its construction required nearly a year, involving the labor of at least fifteen subcontractors. This up-to-date structure was chastely clad in red brick and cast stone in a vaguely Renaissance style, masking the modern technologies at its core.[31]

Across town, at the edge of the expanding civic center, an edifice of equal prominence and similar cost went up at the same time. Ratcliff had received the commission for the Berkeley Elks Club as the result of a design competition. His first essay in a monumental Beaux-Arts mode, it was also his first building in reinforced concrete, a modern material much in vogue after the earthquake.[32] He molded the structure into a somber classicist block with a giant order of pilasters on the principal façade. The building's quiet dignity reflected its internal function as a private club

Glen Garry Apartments, Ridge Road and LeRoy Avenue, Berkeley, 1912; demolished. Located a block north of campus, Ratcliff's first large apartment building had a Secessionist flavor. The university redeveloped the site in the 1960s.

Channing Apartments, College Avenue, Berkeley, 1913. Reprising elements of the Hearst Memorial Mining Building, the Channing stands as a monument to the enduring partnership of Walter H. Ratcliff and Charles Louis McFarland.

SKETCH FOR ELKS CLUB AT BERKELEY CALIF

Elks Club, Allston Way, Berkeley, 1914. The rendering is by
Chesley Bonestall, who later became a noted astronomical artist.

for civic leaders as well as its external function as a contributor to a City Beautiful ensemble that included a large Renaissance Revival post office, built that same year on an adjoining parcel.[33]

The completion of another prestigious club commission was feted with a Christmas banquet in 1914. The Commercial Club occupied the top two floors of the fourteen-story Merchants' Exchange Building, a celebrated San Francisco skyscraper that had survived the earthquake and fire; Ratcliff's remodeling of these floors created the feeling of a posh London club high above the city streets. The transition from the cold marble of the elevator lobby to the wood-paneled vestibule of the club, with its beamed ceiling and fireplace, was startling. A wide staircase wound up to a library, lounge, and large dining room on the top floor; carved mahogany, molded plaster, ample fireplaces, and fine furnishings were used throughout. To the English-born architect and critic B. J. S. Cahill, the club had the "simple

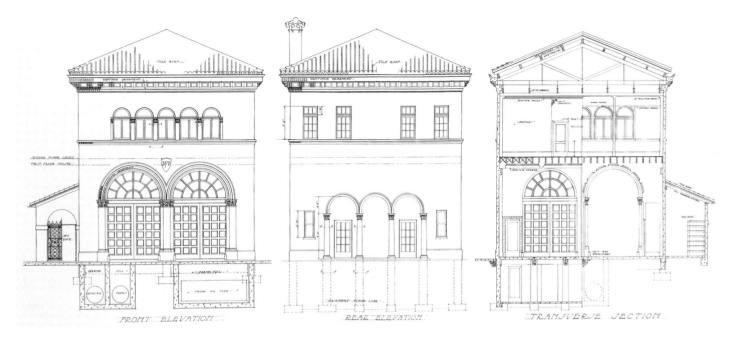

ABOVE: *Elevations and section, Fire Station No. 2, Berkeley.*
RIGHT: *Fire Station No. 2, Durant Avenue, Berkeley, 1914;
demolished. Built as the city's central station, this downtown
landmark was razed for a parking lot in the 1960s.*

elegance of a gentleman's home . . . instinct with
fine feeling and extraordinary good taste. We
think that there is no other club house on the
coast more charmingly designed nor more nicely
adapted to its proper purpose."[34]

Another signal achievement of this period was
Ratcliff's appointment, in September 1913, to the
post of Berkeley city architect, a showcase for his
talents no less prominent than the commissions he
was receiving on both sides of the bay.[35] During his
seven years in the position, which he held concurrently with his private practice, he performed his
duties as designer, planner, estimator, adviser, and
administrator with effective practicality. As much

as it cemented his reputation in Berkeley, the job enhanced his standing within the profession.

Since the earthquake, Berkeley's government had been struggling to cope with demands placed on the city's infrastructure and municipal services by the burgeoning population and geographical expansion. In 1913, voters approved $570,000 in bonds for new sewers and fire stations. "Since it was necessary to erect the firehouses in residential sections of the City, the Council felt it a duty to have them harmonize as much as possible with the surrounding buildings, and, in order to carry out this idea, created the office of City Architect," stated the city's annual report for 1914. "Mr. W. H. Ratcliff, Jr., who was appointed City Architect, immediately prepared plans and specifications."[36]

Erected in 1914, the four new firehouses included neighborhood stations in the Northside, Southside, and Claremont, as well as a larger main station downtown. The Claremont and downtown stations shared the classicized stucco-and-tile idiom favored by the architect, with roughcast veneers, clay tile roofs, and round-arched doorways and windows. The Southside station, with its gable roof and rows of casement windows, was more residential in feeling. Ratcliff also designed the city's new corporation yard—a compound of garages and sheds for vehicle and equipment storage—using a red-brick Tudor style for the complex.[37]

In 1914, Berkeley voters also approved $500,000 in bonds for five new schools, having rejected a $1.3 million school-bond measure earlier that year. Ratcliff supervised the design process for the board of education; his report, adopted in January 1915, analyzed programmatic requirements and costs, arriving at remarkably low construction figures within the constraints of the reduced bond issue. He proceeded to design the largest of the schools, Thomas Edison, advising the board on the selection of four firms for the other designs. Each firm came up with a structural and stylistic solution within the parameters of the program and budget worked out by Ratcliff. Construction on the five schools was brought to completion in 1916.[38]

Ratcliff's discussion of Edison School in the *Architect and Engineer* gave a glimpse of his pragmatic methods: "The total cost of the building was $71,090, or about $7,000 less than the amount allowed by the Council. The contracts for this building were segregated and let separately at a considerable saving to the city. The price of 9.49 cents per cubic foot sets a new price record for Class C [brick] schools." As it turned out, his was the only school to utilize brick construction instead of cheaper wood framing. Edison's brick walls were tied with steel girders and reinforced concrete columns; mullioned bay windows and ornamental cast-stone trim evoked a Tudor feeling, with the wings achieving harmony through their shared palette and styling.[39]

During his tenure as city architect Ratcliff also served on the eleven-member civic art commission, created by the city council "to provide for and regulate the future growth and development of Berkeley." Established in 1915, with Duncan McDuffie as its first president, this was one of the first city planning commissions in the state. In 1916, the commission produced one of the state's first zoning codes.[40]

WALTER RATCLIFF became a successful and respected architect within five years of opening his office in Berkeley. In the banner year of 1914, when he designed his residence as well as his first large building, his first major project in San Francisco, and his first public buildings as city architect, he was honored with the first published retrospective of his work. A drawing of the Berkeley Elks Club graced the cover of the October 1914 issue of the *Architect and Engineer,* the region's leading architectural journal, which devoted twenty pages of the issue to Ratcliff's recent buildings.[41] The article began with the observation that most architects did not like being typecast as residential designers, preferring the prestige and profit accruing from larger commissions: "Ask ten architects who have achieved fame as designers of homes if they specialize in domestic architecture and nine of them will tell you they do not." Despite the professional state of denial, the writer concluded, a noteworthy tradition of residential design had taken hold in California; among the architects cited were Irving Gill and Greene & Greene, in southern California, and Bernard Maybeck, Louis Christian Mullgardt, Edgar Mathews, William Knowles, and Albert Farr, in the Bay Area.

> In Berkeley you will hear about W. H. Ratcliff, Jr., but Mr. Ratcliff, like some of the other men whose names I have just mentioned, does not enthuse when you speak to him about his tendency towards domestic architecture. "It's bread and butter with me," is his rather frank way of expressing, or rather excusing himself. To this he adds a consoling paragraph: "You can't design a million-dollar office building or a monumental bank structure if you don't get the commission, can you?"

The sense of frustration in these words—the evident ambition to work on a larger scale—had begun to be assuaged by projects like the Elks Club and the Cambridge Apartments, views of which appeared in the article. The article also included pictures of the Glen Garry and Channing Apartments, and it gave in-depth coverage to the Head, Breed, Shearman, and Nickerson residences.

More articles were published over the next few years. B. J. S. Cahill's lavishly illustrated piece on the Commercial Club and his laudatory lead article about Berkeley's new schools both appeared in 1916. "The city of Berkeley is to be congratulated on a feat of school building without parallel on the Pacific Coast," Cahill said in the latter article, praising Ratcliff's cost-effective management of the program. "By just what process the Berkeley authorities chose a really first-class man for city architect I personally do not know."

The flurry of published work after 1914 marked the high point of Ratcliff's pre–World War I career as a Berkeley architect. His reputation, based equally on good sense and good design, was beginning to grow beyond the confines of his home city. He was as yet primarily a designer of residences, with a small but impressive portfolio of other commissions. Over the coming decade, as his practice entered its most productive phase, a series of major projects for academic, ecclesiastical, and commercial clients would place him among the leading Bay Area architects of his generation.

Three Arrival and Survival

IN 1919, Walter Ratcliff resumed his active practice after a two-year hiatus brought on by the exigencies of war. Few jobs had come through the office since 1916, and there was little prospect for work in the lingering postwar recession. Though his practice would be lifted to new levels of productivity by the buoyant economy of 1920s America, he didn't yet know that; like every other architect and builder, he had to ride out the bad times, trusting they would get better. The faltering economy underscored the gloom of those postwar years. The carnage in Europe and the ensuing flu pandemic, which claimed more lives than the trenches, had undermined the utopian optimism of the West. America entered an era of heightened cynicism and corruption, of ethnic and racial strife, of Prohibition and the gangland violence it spawned in the nation's rapidly growing, industrialized cities. In seminaries from Boston to Berkeley, millenarian hope gave way to more chastened creeds as the fiery rant of revivalism—back-to-basics, "old-time" religion—resounded across the land.

In this turbulent and fearful postwar climate, the upsurge of revivalist architecture, like revivalist religion, formed part of a broad-based conservative reaction—a retreat from modernity in an increasingly chaotic world. Residential subdivisions came to resemble historical theme parks, olios of Period Revival styles evoking Norman France, Tudor England, Colonial America, Spanish California, and so forth. Apartment buildings, schools, libraries, churches, banks, stores, and even factories spread the revivalist vocabulary into every corner of the urban landscape. What distinguished the wide run of new buildings from their prewar predecessors was a more literal and pictorial sense of the past, often making them seem like stage sets.

This pervasive craving for fantasy and escape drove popular culture and drew sustenance from it in a kind of endless feedback loop. The cinema, a newly mature art form of great power, mesmerized audiences with historical romances of such technical brilliance that they seemed able to transport the viewer back to ancient Baghdad, Spanish California, or any other place of the filmmaker's choosing. Small wonder that revivalist architecture flourished in this milieu: it translated the flickering, dreamlike visions of the screen into the habitations of the daytime world.

California, the premier manufacturer of fantasy, far from the front lines of war and crime, its few million residents basking in a mountain-ringed, ocean-facing, sun-drenched sanctuary, managed to avoid the darker impulses of the era. The Golden State retained its luster, and the Bay Area remained an extraordinarily pleasant place to live, its towns and cities encompassed by orchards, hills, and water. But the Bay Area wasn't immune to the fluctuations of the economy or the ravages of disease. After the war, shipyards closed, canneries cut back, offices shrank; men and women lost their jobs, and many more lost their lives to influenza.[1]

In the 1920s, a quickening economy would give rise to many thousands of new buildings, imprinting the region with revivalist imagery. Progressive architects all made the shift to one degree or another. Maybeck, now in his sixties, dabbled in Spanish revivalism as his output dwindled over the course of the decade; the same held true for

South elevation of the Holbrook Library (now the Badè Museum), Pacific School of Religion, Scenic Avenue, Berkeley, 1926.

Coxhead. John Hudson Thomas, the polymath of prewar progressivism, withdrew into a storybook medievalism. Julia Morgan continued producing pitch-perfect exercises in eclecticism as she labored on her masterwork at San Simeon. Yet the attention she lavished on materials and workmanship, imbued with a pre-industrial romanticism, also attested to an abiding Arts and Crafts sensibility. In this she was emulated by East Bay architects like Carr Jones and William Raymond Yelland, whose finely wrought medieval fantasies owed as much to the Arts and Crafts ethos of the 1890s as the revivalist impulses of the 1920s.

During the 1920s, Berkeley's population would grow by 50 percent, to over eighty thousand—a fivefold increase since the turn of the century— while university enrollment passed the milestone of ten thousand. Revivalist buildings proliferated, and the campus itself took on revivalist overtones.[2]

Disaster played a role in Berkeley's makeover. A late summer fire in 1923 swept down the Northside hills and consumed hundreds of houses, destroying in a single day a famous Arts and Crafts enclave three decades in the making. Within a few years, revivalist buildings would blanket the area, including some of Ratcliff's most memorable work.

WALTER H. RATCLIFF, Jr., turned 38 in 1919, on the cusp of his second decade of independent practice. One wonders how he responded to the anxiety of the times. Whatever the assaults on his temperament, whatever his trauma over what had befallen England, he had a family to care for and a business to tend. Work remained scarce, but the

Mary Kingsley house, Cedar Street and Euclid Avenue, Berkeley, 1924. Work started on the house within weeks of the September 1923 fire, remnants of which are still visible. The Humphrey and Read house (right) was built concurrently. These two houses were among Ratcliff's earliest residential designs in the postwar Spanish revivalist mode.

family had grown—besides Robert and Peter, the Ratcliffs now had two more children, Margaret and their baby, Muriel, who was born in the spring of 1919, six months after the Armistice.

As his practice languished, Ratcliff found time to give architectural expression to his feelings about the war. His rendering for a memorial building in Oakland, published soon after Muriel's birth, depicted a marble-clad mausoleum with a domed rotunda and colonnaded wings stretching three hundred and fifty feet along Lake Merritt. Its plan included an auditorium, banquet hall, war museum, and rooms for visiting veterans. Prepared at the behest of an enthusiastic but underfunded citizen group, this ideal Beaux-Arts scheme remained a symbolic gesture, unbuilt.[3] Meanwhile,

the architect picked up work wherever he could find it. His most reliable client at the time was George E. Billings, a Marin County sportsman and longtime tennis partner. Billings owned insurance and shipping companies in San Francisco, and he had been instrumental in Ratcliff's getting the Commercial Club job. In 1918, he provided the architect with a rare wartime commission, a four-story brick warehouse on the San Francisco waterfront. The following year, he commissioned two small office buildings in downtown San Francisco; the two- and three-story buildings faced each other across California Street, a few blocks east of the Merchants' Exchange Building.[4]

Ratcliff also continued in his position as Berkeley city architect, though that work had dried up after the flurry of jobs in 1914 and 1915. Then, in 1919, a new bond issue led to commissions for a school and a gymnasium. Early in 1921, as the school was under construction, the city council abolished the post of city architect as a cost-saving measure.[5]

Later that year, Ratcliff's old friend and associate McFarland devised a new business arrangement that would provide both men with financial security for the foreseeable future. They had collaborated on relatively few design and construction ventures since their last speculative house for Alameda County Home Builders, in 1916. That firm, renamed Fidelity Mortgage Securities Company of California in 1918, built a handful of speculative bungalows after the war, but otherwise dealt primarily in construction loans. The two men still had their offices on the same floor of the First National Bank Building.[6]

McFarland's new focus on financing culminated in the August 1921 incorporation of the Fidelity Guaranty Building and Loan Association, with himself as president, Ratcliff as vice-president, and seven other investors on the board of directors. Bearing the motto "Six Percent and Safety," the institution functioned as a savings and lending bank, paying interest on deposits that in turn provided the funds for home-purchase and construction loans issued at a higher rate. Fidelity Guaranty was the first of several building and loan associations established in Berkeley in the 1920s, and it rode the wave of the construction boom. The company's assets soared from $130,000 at the time of its founding to $1.9 million in 1926, exceeding $3.5 million by the end of the decade.[7]

McFarland's management of the bank left Ratcliff free to pursue his architectural career, which reached its high point in the 1920s. Around the time Fidelity was started, he moved up to the fifth floor of the First National Bank Building, where Howard had once had his office. Berkeley remained the locus of his practice, but the projects grew larger and costlier, including clubs, schools, churches, parish halls, banks, office buildings, apartment buildings, fraternity and sorority houses, and a wide array of projects for institutions of higher learning. He had begun to take on such jobs before the war, but they had been the exceptions, not the rule, in his primarily residential practice.

Residential designs had accounted for over three-fourths of Ratcliff's prewar commissions; now they comprised less than a fourth. Approximately fifty houses came out of the office in the twenty-seven years between the end of World War I and the end of World War II—fewer houses than the architect had designed in his first three years of independent practice. Speculative jobs, a major source of work in the prewar years, virtually ceased after 1919, when Ratcliff designed a cluster of nine bungalows in south Berkeley for the Fidelity Securities Mortgage Company and a second cluster of eight bungalows in north Oakland, near the Berkeley border, for another investor. From that point on, nearly all of the firm's houses would be for individual homeowners, and all would be designed as variations on English and Spanish revivalist themes.

IN NO area of Walter Ratcliff's practice was the shift in emphasis more dramatic than commercial architecture, a reflection both of the boom times

Elmwood Branch, Mercantile Trust Company, College and Ashby Avenues, Berkeley, 1925. Its tile-roofed repose quickened by a spring of arches, the prominently sited bank (now Wells Fargo) functions both as an anchor to the Elmwood commercial district and as a gateway to Claremont.

and of his enhanced stature within Berkeley's business community. In the 1920s and 1930s, his commercial output in Berkeley would total over a dozen projects, and no other architect of his generation would have an equivalent impact on the evolving look and feel of the downtown and civic center.

Among the architect's commissions were buildings for his own company and for his business associates. The new offices of the Fidelity Guaranty Building and Loan Association opened to the public in May 1926. Called a "beautiful new temple of finance" by the local press, the concrete structure had an arcaded front trimmed with limestone; inside, the trussed wood ceiling was inscribed with handpainted homilies calculated

Fidelity Building, Shattuck Avenue, Berkeley, 1926. The offices of the Fidelity Guaranty Building and Loan Association, and of the Fidelity Mortgage Securities Company, were located here. Ratcliff employed a stucco-and-tile idiom for other commercial projects of the period.

to induce thrift in the hearts of the customers ("Hard work and saving is the road to prosperity: there is no other—Benjamin Franklin"; "If you would be sure you are beginning right, begin to save—Theodore Roosevelt").[8] Ratcliff's 1926 alterations and additions to the Shattuck Hotel, for J. F. Hink and Son, Berkeley's family-owned department store, included elegant shopping arcades, a lofty new emporium, and a private roof garden with penthouse apartment for the owner, Lester Hink (who would later serve as a Fidelity director). The glass-enclosed offices of the Mason-McDuffie Company, opened in May 1929, felt like a showroom displaying the transparent drive of the real estate men who worked there; concrete piers with handcrafted capitals framed the big windows.[9]

Ratcliff's ultimate commercial commission was the $500,000 Chamber of Commerce Building. This twelve-story skyscraper, Berkeley's first, was his biggest project prior to World War II. The developer was the Central Berkeley Building Company, one of whose directors, F. Linden Naylor, sat on the board of the Fidelity Guaranty Building and Loan Association. Another director was the vice-president of the Mercantile Trust Company, soon to become the American Trust Company, a bank that assumed ownership of the building while it was still under construction. Fidelity director John W. Havens sat on that bank's advisory board. The building was named in honor of the organization whose offices would occupy the twelfth floor, though it would be more commonly known as the American Trust Building.[10]

Ground was broken for the structure in the

Chamber of Commerce Building, Shattuck Avenue, Berkeley, 1927. Commonly known as the American Trust Building, this was Berkeley's first skyscraper. The First National Bank Building (left) is partially visible across Center Street.

event of the decade. Four months after the opening, American Trust commissioned a $100,000 remodeling of the ground floor for a banking hall; Ratcliff's redesign gave the base an arcaded treatment echoing the First National Bank Building.

The structure incorporated a steel frame, reinforced concrete floors, steel-lath partitions, brick curtain walls, and terra-cotta trim. Mechanical systems included elevators serving an underground garage and customized services (plumbing, electrical, and compressed air) to three floors intended for dentists' offices. The exterior design followed precedent in its three-part vertical composition reprising the base, shaft, and capital of a classical column. The Renaissance styling displayed a rich palette of colors: brown, tan, orange, and ochre bricks blending to produce a deep russet color for the shaft, set off by the faux-granite terra-cotta of the base and a cream terra-cotta topping. The ornate banking hall and elevator lobby were finished in marble.

The Chamber of Commerce Building was a dominant new element on the city's skyline, a tower of commerce vying with the celebrated tower of learning on the nearby campus. At the building's dedication, Robert G. Sproul, vice-president of the university, had spoken of "those who opposed the erection of this building, saying that it obstructed the university's view of the Golden Gate and was not a wise thing for the city." The skyscraper's visual impact on the campus was not severe, however; the campus occupied higher ground, and its iconic Campanile rose to twice the height of the new tower.[11]

summer of 1925, and the building formally opened with fireworks and speeches in January 1927. Situated at the northwest corner of Shattuck Avenue and Center Street, it towered over the First National Bank Building on the opposite corner. Though buildings of similar height had long since risen in the region's two commercial centers—in San Francisco as early as the 1890s, in Oakland by 1910—for downtown Berkeley it was the signal

The University of California provided Ratcliff with several downtown commissions in the latter half of the 1920s, including a print shop, garage, and automobile showroom. Intended for lease to commercial tenants, these buildings were clustered at the east edge of the commercial district, across from the campus. The architect's best-known university project was on the campus itself. Opened in 1928, Morrison Library was a redesign of the old reserve book room in Doe Memorial Library. The alterations were funded by May Treat Morrison (Class of 1878), who

Morrison Library, University of California, Berkeley, 1928.

also provided the furnishings along with her late husband's library of fifteen thousand volumes. In the manner of the Commercial Club, the library had the luxuriant feeling of a sitting room in a manor house, elegantly finished in golden oak wainscoting and a carved plaster ceiling with brass chandeliers. It remains a favored room on campus for receptions and special events.[12]

Elevator lobby, Chamber of Commerce Building. The ornate plaster and marble finish was reprised in the banking hall.

*Pacific School of Religion, Scenic Avenue, Berkeley, 1926. Now known
as the Holbrook Building, the former Administration Building and
Charles Holbrook Library is the centerpiece of the campus.*

As RATCLIFF established himself in the downtown and campus environments, he worked on other important projects in and around Berkeley. And while his commercial work was rendered in an eclectic mode tending toward classicism, also evident in Morrison Library, his designs for clubhouses, seminaries, and churches embraced an English vocabulary. Ratcliff's essays in English revivalism acquired increasing suavity in his larger and costlier commissions of the 1920s. The Berkeley Country Club (1921), perched on a hilltop in El Cerrito several miles north of the city, was composed of three lightly half-timbered gabled wings with prominent chimneys, loosely enclosing a garden. In this building the architect created his first great hall in the English style— vaulted space spanned by wood trusses—a signature of his mature work.[13]

Ratcliff's principal achievement in the English mode was the series of projects he completed for seminaries and churches in the Northside following the 1923 fire. Commissions from the Pacific School of Religion, Church Divinity School of the Pacific, University Christian Church, and Starr King School for the Ministry allowed the architect to remold the burned-over, formerly residential hilltop around Ridge Road, Scenic Avenue, and LeConte Avenue into a brick-and-stone setting with the look of a long-established academic community—the architectural foundation of what came to be known as Holy Hill, locus sanctorum of the Graduate Theological Union.[14]

Ratcliff drew from English sources, primarily Gothic, for his work on the hill. His choice of a Gothic idiom for these buildings, perched above the proud classicist campus on their flank, was an appropriate response to the program. It made a revivalist statement about the primacy of theology over other arts and sciences: the credo of the medieval mind and the antithesis of classical reason. The irony, of course, was that self-reliant rationalism had by then supplanted faith in liberal seminaries like the Pacific School of Religion. In this light, the architect's evocative medievalism was a form of romantic idealism, serving the needs of clients whose hope in humanity had been vitiated by the war and whose faith in reason was itself in crisis.[15]

The centerpiece of Holy Hill was the new campus of the Pacific School of Religion (PSR), the oldest seminary in the western United States. Located in a former hotel in Berkeley's Southside since 1901, the school had later purchased land on Piedmont Avenue, at the east edge of the campus. In 1922, under the deanship of William Frederic Badè, the trustees had hired Ratcliff to design the new building.[16]

The planned project received national attention. A Boston newspaper commented favorably on the design: "One of the leading architects of the coast, Mr. Walter H. Ratcliff, has been engaged as architect and is preparing plans for a structure which promises to be one of the most attractive and successful buildings of the kind in the country."[17] The site was abandoned, however, after the 1923 fire, in part because the university coveted the property for its own expansion plans. The seminary trustees were persuaded to sell once they found another site: a hilltop parcel formerly owned by Phoebe Apperson Hearst, one block

Bird's-eye rendering of Ratcliff's proposed campus for the Pacific School of Religion, 1923.

north of the campus. Situated at the west end of Ridge Road between Arch Street and LeConte and Scenic Avenues, the property was one of the most beautiful in Berkeley; it commanded its setting like a promontory on an urban sea, with a panoptic view of the hills, campus, city, and bay. Wooded slopes loomed large; to the west was the Golden Gate.[18]

In December 1923, three months after the fire, Ratcliff produced a schematic plan for the new site.[19] The campus was conceived as an axial ensemble of two open quadrangles, loosely modeled on the cloistered colleges of Oxford and Cambridge. The chapel and the library, flanking the main entrance to the campus, were the most elaborately conceived. The chapel, with its enframed window and vertical buttresses, recalled fifteenth-century English Perpendicular Gothic churches, such as King's College Chapel at Cambridge. The library (the front ell of the main building) echoed the chapel in its overall treatment. The administrative and classroom wings mixed Gothic arcades and Tudor bays; the dormitories were similar in feeling.

Only a fragment of this ambitious plan—the north section of the main building, with library, and one dormitory building—was completed, early in 1926, following a year of construction. At the dedication ceremonies for the library, President Herman F. Swartz bestowed on Ratcliff an honorary Master of Arts degree. "Mr. Ratcliff has been an earnest and sympathetic student of the desires of the donor of this building [and] the trustees and faculty of the Pacific School of Religion," said one speaker. "He has created and built in the spirit of the architects of the great churches of the earlier centuries. He has visioned the larger whole and has sought to build worthily and adequately for the new day that is dawning so rapidly. Nurtured in a home of religious devotion, he has caught and incarnated in these buildings the atmosphere that should pervade the Pacific School of Religion."[20]

As built, the Administration Building and Charles Holbrook Library, as it was known then, had a linear plan with short wings, or ells, projecting at the ends.[21] The library wing was the one element of the original scheme that did not go through major revision. Its veneer of rusticated golden-gray stone incorporated finial-topped buttresses and smooth panels embossed with symbols of the faith. The remainder of the building was sheathed in a fine dense brick variegated both tonally, in shades of ochre, orange, red, purple, and brown, and texturally, through an admixture of misshapen clinkers. Inlaid stone provided random accents to the brick, also serving as trim for windows, buttresses, and quoins.

Slate roofing, copper downspouts, and oak doors strapped with iron added to the material richness.[22]

The Men's Hall (now Benton Hall), situated diagonally across the green from the Holbrook Building, was more understated, with lightly half-timbered stucco veneer and stone entry arches. A mullioned bay loomed above the hillside on Arch Street—an element that conveyed a sense of monastic retreat while accentuating this less frequently seen face of the campus.

The Pacific School of Religion, as it appears today, pieced together over five decades, is a mix of modern and traditional. Ratcliff's two buildings anchor the complex in strata of time both real and imagined. In the former library, a luminous space encompassed by Gothic windows and spanned by graceful trusses, continuity with the past is strongly present. If there remains something poignant in Ratcliff's achievement in this great hall—an almost palpable sense of what the completed campus might have been—here, at least, his vision was fully realized.

THE SECOND seminary to open on Holy Hill was the Church Divinity School of the Pacific (CDSP). Founded in 1894 by the Episcopal Church for the training of ministers in dioceses west of the Rockies, the school moved from San Mateo to San Francisco after the 1906 earthquake. The prospect of collegiality with PSR and the University of California persuaded the trustees to move across the bay to Berkeley.

In the summer of 1926, six months after PSR occupied its new campus, CDSP acquired a sizable parcel fronting on Ridge Road between Euclid and LeConte Avenues, "one block away from the north gate of the university in one direction and one block away from the Pacific School of Religion in the other," according to the school history.[23] The sloping property took in the site of several houses destroyed in the 1923 fire; two were by John Galen Howard, including his own 1903 residence. Once funds were raised, Ratcliff was commissioned to design a building to house classrooms, offices, and dormitory rooms. Students and faculty moved into newly completed Gibbs Hall in April 1930. The Ratcliff office would design two more buildings on Ridge Road for CDSP. East of Gibbs Hall was Dean's House (1934), later known as Shires Hall, which served as the residence of the school's director; uphill, to the west, was All Saints' Chapel (1937), enlarged in 1940 with a rear addition for the school library.

The buildings stepped up the hillside in an unpretentious manner, set back from the palm-lined street behind stone retaining walls and manicured lawns in a way that recalled the residential neighborhood they had replaced. They shared a palette of red brick, sparse stone trim, and slate roofs in a more or less Tudor styling that evoked the Anglican roots of the denomination. Gibbs Hall, with its steep buttressed gables, two-story bay of leaded casements, and stone-framed entry, was the centerpiece of the group. A Gothic arcade connected it to the small Gothic chapel. Shires Hall was the simplest of the three, its gabled form softened by a quaint entry porch.[24]

Walter Ratcliff's final commissions on Holy Hill were University Christian Church and Starr

King School for the Ministry, on adjoining lots at the corner of LeConte and Scenic Avenues, facing both PSR and CDSP. University Christian Church was built by the Disciples of Christ, a denomination with close ties to PSR. Dedicated in the spring of 1931, the building—Ratcliff's largest church—fronted on Scenic Avenue across from the Holbrook Library. Its English Gothic styling, dominated by a buttressed and crenellated entry tower, together with its veneer of red brick and buff stone trim, set up harmonies with both of the seminaries it bordered. The church's sanctuary was another of Ratcliff's great vaulted rooms, quite different in feeling from the Holbrook Library; here the dimly lit space was spanned by massive trusses that were steeply pitched and roughly finished, more evocative of tenebrous mystery and yearning than the calm, contained curves of the library.

The Unitarian-Universalist Starr King School for the Ministry opened in 1941 next door to University Christian Church. With its low façade of red brick in no particular style, the building fit unobtrusively into its setting, in similar manner to a small, concurrent addition at the Pacific School of Religion—discreet codas to the architect's nearly twenty-year opus on Holy Hill.

THAT THE Pacific School of Religion had increased Ratcliff's command of English Gothic and Tudor revivalism was evident in the more supple confidence he brought to later commissions. By contrast, his early postwar houses in the English mode had felt muted and withdrawn, almost fortress-like, as if in reaction to the

Hillside School, LeRoy Avenue and Buena Vista Way, Berkeley. The building's resemblance to a Tudor streetscape is evident in this historic view, taken soon after the school opened in 1926.

troubled times. They also partook of the characteristic dryness of architecture of the period: shrunken eaves, austere façades, sober touches of detailing: Prohibition-era houses par excellence. The Floyd house (1920), near the Claremont Hotel, stood stiffly on its corner site, its roof pulled down like a helmet, its chimney as erect as a gun, its entry defensively squeezed between columns under a blind arch, its oriel window suspended like a sentry post. The pseudo-thatch roof was softened with rounded ridges, intricate shinglework, and eaves that undulated quaintly over windows, but here the gesture felt hollow.

Within a few years, Ratcliff's English revivalism opened up and ripened. This was particularly evident in larger commissions. These buildings shared certain features, such as half-timbering, slate-covered gable roofs, and chimneys of varying size and elaboration, and each included a hall as its principal interior feature. The hall was typically a vaulted space with wood-paneled ceiling, open wood trusses, and a fireplace, illuminated by large windows.

The "great hall" and "big window" came to characterize Ratcliff's mature English mode, as in his addition to the Berkeley Country Club and his parish hall for St. Mark's (now All Souls) Episcopal Church, both of 1924. Westminster House, erected in 1926 by the Presbyterian Church for student outreach, occupied a prominent Southside corner facing the campus, where College Avenue meets Bancroft Way. It recalled the recently completed Men's Hall at the Pacific School of Religion, though with finer detailing, including pleated and corbelled brick chimneys, plank doors with bronzed knockers, and extensive leaded glass. The large social hall was finished in paneled oak, thick beams, and tall windows with stone trim.[25]

Hillside School, built in 1925 and 1926 to replace a school of that name lost in the Northside fire, was one of several commissions Ratcliff received for schools and school additions in the 1920s. Hillside was crisply composed as a linear series of gabled sections, conveying the feeling of a compacted medieval village on its narrow upland site. Generously scaled ranks of windows were set into the sections, notably the great mullioned panel of the auditorium. The school exuded a whiff of fantasy, a slightly off-kilter distortion of proportion and scale suggestive of dream.[26]

Berkeley Day Nursery, Sixth Street, Berkeley, 1927. The big window serves one of the building's two assembly halls; entry porch on right.

The Berkeley Day Nursery of 1927, a progressive forerunner of the modern day-care center, was one of Ratcliff's final essays in the half-timbered mode, and one of his most charming.[27] In this building, situated in west Berkeley, far removed from the city center, an element of fantasy prevailed. The building was gently scaled down and infused with storybook effects as if to accommodate the children who were to spend time there. The slate gables were pulled low, like pegged tents, forcing wall-dormers to pop up through the drooping eaves. The obvious appliqué of wavy half-timbering enhanced the feeling of make-believe produced by the dollhouse porch. Inside, walls met ceilings in smooth curves, and the two redwood halls were child-sized, with low trusses and a miniature fireplace.

Fantasy also appeared in Ratcliff's English houses of the period. In the residence of Edmond and Edith Vernon O'Neill, built next door to the Ratcliff home on Roble Road in the winter of 1925, half-timbered and brick veneers were combined with quaintly bowed roofs and a mammoth brick chimney to achieve an evocative pastiche.[28] Ratcliff's 1926 residence in Thousand Oaks for F. Linden Naylor, a director of Fidelity

F. Linden Naylor house, Somerset Place, Berkeley, 1926. Among Ratcliff's best-known revivalist houses, the storybook residence was designed for a business partner.

Guaranty, produced an effect both picturesque and pictorial, like a period illustration from a book of fairy tales. A multigabled composition with lushly rendered surfaces of soft stucco, rustic stone, polychrome slate, rough-hewn wood, and leaded glass, this tactile house captured the feeling of "an unreal stage-set fantasy by segmenting the building into distinct separate volumes and by carefully scaling everything down, including the walled garden and cobblestone stepping stones which lead to the house."[29] Adjoined by living and dining rooms, the beamed entry hall opened directly onto a rear terrace looking over the garden, a recurring plan in Ratcliff's residential work.

A larger house of like whimsy was built in the Northside burn zone in 1929 for the mining engineer George D. Blood.[30] The Blood mansion combined materials of variegated color and texture (pastel stucco, dark-stained half-timbering, red brick, white stone, multihued slate) with distorted and exaggerated proportions—steep gables, spreading slopes, towering chimney, sequestered entry. In the living room, everything seemed a bit too big,

Entrance hall of Naylor house. Low, beamed ceilings, irregular plaster, carved newels, and quaint hardware sustained the atmosphere of medieval fantasy.

from the pointy trusses of the lofty ceiling to the gaping window on the far wall, evoking a vertiginous feeling of space from a child's perspective. Yet one also sensed in this house, as in the Naylor house, a devotion to materials, workmanship, and landscaping rooted in Berkeley's Arts and Crafts tradition.

OVER THE course of the 1920s, as Walter Ratcliff applied himself to mastering the nuances of English revivalism, he became equally adept in the newly popular Spanish Colonial Revival style. In the same way that the commission for the Pacific School of Religion had honed his skills as an English revivalist, his appointment to the post of campus architect at Mills College allowed him to experiment with Spanish revivalism on a large scale. He acquired a fluency in the idiom that

would serve him well for the remainder of his career.

With its basic vocabulary of white stucco walls and red tile roofs, and its standardized trim palette of wrought iron, ceramic tile, stone, and wood, Spanish revivalism was more readily assimilated by the architectural profession and more easily accepted by the public than any other style trend of the period. This was due in part to the widely held belief that Spanish imagery was the most apt response to the region's history—that it was, in effect, a regional style—and in part to its air of unforced familiarity. After all, similar images and impulses had informed Bay Area architecture since the late nineteenth century, and people had grown accustomed to the stucco-and-tile idiom. All of this meant that Spanish revivalism became the most commonly encountered historicist style in the Bay Area between the two world wars.

The style was invented, or reinvented, by the Boston architect Bertram Goodhue for the San Diego Panama-California Exposition, staged in 1915 to celebrate the opening of the Panama Canal. When Goodhue, one of the country's ablest practitioners of academic eclecticism, received the commission for the exposition—a job he coveted as a showcase for his talents—he seized the occasion to launch a revival deemed suitable for California. Spanish Baroque buildings of the seventeenth and eighteenth centuries served as the primary source for the lush sculptural treatment of his doorways, windows, and towers, in vivid contrast to unadorned stucco walls and tile roofs.

These exposition buildings represented the latest iteration, if not the culmination, of the

Harry Unna house, Tamalpais Road, Berkeley, 1925. One of Ratcliff's larger Spanish revivalist houses, the L-plan residence (seen here from the rear garden) was built on the site of Maybeck's 1907 Underhill house ("El Toyon"), a casualty of the 1923 fire.

decades-long effort to revive Spanish Colonial motifs that had begun in the 1880s with Mission Revival. The older style, inspired by eighteenth- and nineteenth-century missions in California and the Southwest, had largely remained an appliqué architecture of stucco-clad façades trimmed with tile and embellished with standardized motifs such as curved parapets and round arches.[31] By going to the source, to Spain herself, Goodhue reinvigorated the tradition, which would broaden in the 1920s to run a gamut of Mediterranean sources, from Andalusian villages and Tuscan villas to Moroccan medinas.[32] In the end, the stucco-and-

Claude H. McEntyre house, Avalon Avenue, Berkeley, 1928. This view shows the entrance court, adjoined by a stage-set balcony with cascading stairs. The Claremont house is planned around an interior courtyard.

tile mode transcended its particular sources to become a stylistic shorthand that was applied to every conceivable type of building, from gas stations to churches. The irony, for some, was that this latest California fad had been launched by an East Coast designer; but Goodhue merely followed in the paths of Maybeck and Howard, master illusionists who had imported invented histories to a place without a past, a state not yet seventy-five years old.[33]

Ratcliff had used stucco veneers and tile roofs in some of his prewar designs, notably his own residence. Yet these motifs never comprised a dominant strain, serving more as a tonality than a style. After World War I, a standardized Spanish revivalism began to pervade his work, vying for dominance with his Englishness. This new style owed as much to Goodhue as it did to his own intellectual curiosity. Ratcliff reportedly went to the San Diego fair, and in 1922, in a rare trip outside the country, he traveled to Mexico to study colonial buildings.[34] His large library included books on Goodhue and works on Spanish and Mexican architecture, and the professional journals he subscribed to frequently published photographs of buildings and details of buildings from other countries.

Ratcliff's early postwar forays into Spanish revivalism displayed the same dryness and restraint as his English work of the period. Houses and apartment buildings tended toward rigid symmetry, with flattened surfaces and shrunken elements that seemed muted when compared to his prewar work. These tendencies persisted in the Armstrong Business College, erected in 1923 on a corner parcel behind the Elks Club, at the edge of Berkeley's civic center. The building felt dry, its walls thin. The gabled front maintained symmetry along each of its street façades, with attenuated arched windows on the second story and under-scaled ornament at the entries. In its formality, the building also represented the architect's earnest effort to contribute to the dignity of the civic center, as he had ten years before with the Elks Club. His additions and alterations to the Berkeley High School gymnasium—his last major work in the civic center—exhibited a similar formality.[35]

WALTER RATCLIFF's appointment as campus architect of Mills College in 1921 came at an opportune time.[36] The 40-year-old architect had four young children to support, he had recently been dismissed as city architect of Berkeley, and the postwar economy remained sluggish. The new position would provide a steady flow of projects over the coming decade. In all, Ratcliff's association with Mills College would last twenty-three years, one year longer than John Galen Howard's tenure as supervising architect at the University of California.

The oldest institution of higher education for women on the Pacific Coast, Mills occupied a 140-acre campus at the base of the hills in what was then an outlying section of Oakland. The topography, ranging from meadows and streams to steep wooded slopes, was as varied as the architecture. The campus had opened two years before the University of California. Its centerpiece, Mills Hall, was a sprawling wood structure erected in 1871 in the Second Empire mansard style, and a scattering of other Victorian buildings dotted the grounds. Arrayed around Mills Hall was a distinguished group by Julia Morgan—her celebrated El Campanil bell tower (1904), as well as a library (1906), gymnasium (1909), and social hall (1916). Following the death in 1912 of Morgan's patron Susan Mills, the college's cofounder and longtime president, commissions began passing to other firms, notably Bakewell & Brown. By World War I, the campus presented a casual mix of Victorian and Mission/Mediterranean eclecticism.

Under its new president, Aurelia Henry Reinhardt, who assumed the post in 1916, Mills College embarked on a program of expansion to accommodate growing enrollment. In 1915, Oakland architects Charles W. Dickey and John J. Donovan had produced the college's first master plan, a tightly configured array of buildings in an axial arrangement. The plan did not appeal to the most powerful trustee on the board, Phoebe Hearst, who privately commissioned an alternate scheme from Bernard Maybeck. His elegant layout of boulevards, plazas, and monumental buildings reprised the Beaux-Arts spirit of the Berkeley competition that Hearst had funded and

Ratcliff's original master plan for Mills College, 1921.

Maybeck had directed some twenty years before. The scheme envisioned an entirely new campus, treating the site like a blank canvas with no regard for existing structures (except Morgan's bell tower, which became a focal point of the main axis). Though the trustees formally adopted the plan in 1919, the romantic excess and cost gave them pause; the death of Mrs. Hearst late that same year removed its principal supporter.[37]

In 1921, the trustees turned to Walter H. Ratcliff for yet another iteration of the campus. Submitted that same year, his Mills College Plan reprised Maybeck's Beaux-Arts concept in its salient features, proposing an idealized axial ensemble for the site. The principal buildings were to be grouped along the main parkway off Seminary Avenue. Structures of symbolic and functional importance—a library, a chapel, an art complex—served as the focal points of axial vistas. A music building and an auditorium provided a monumental gateway to the campus from the west. Other buildings were spread across the grounds, including a hilltop dormitory complex and faculty housing near the main gate.

Between 1922 and 1944, Ratcliff would produce drawings for several dozen projects at Mills, including academic buildings, dormitories, faculty housing, support facilities, entrance pylons, and alterations and additions to existing buildings. Much of this work was done in reinforced concrete, the preferred material for new campus buildings due to its fire resistance, durability, and relative economy. While important pieces of Ratcliff's plan were brought to completion, it remained, like the Pacific School of Religion,

ABOVE: *Fine Arts Building, Mills College. Detail of carved wood capital on courtyard corridor, depicting the painter James A. McNeill Whistler.* BELOW: *Fine Arts Building, Mills College, Oakland, 1925, main (south) entrance to gallery wing. A similarly embellished doorway served the north side of the building.*

largely unrealized. The unsurprising decision by the trustees to leave existing facilities in place, in particular Mills Hall and its nimbus of Morgan-designed structures, meant that the contemplated main axis and plaza would never be completed, and that major works like the proposed library and administration building were not likely to be built.

Aurelia Reinhardt had persuaded the trustees that new campus buildings should adhere to the Spanish Colonial Revival style, and Ratcliff's work for the college would hew this line.[38] "One Sunday we met Aurelia Reinhardt at the Oak Knoll Country Club," Peter Ratcliff recalled. "They had just completed their country club building, which was a rather nice colonial Spanish. She said, 'This is the kind of thing I want.' Dad and Mom packed up and went to Mexico."[39]

By 1924, Walter Ratcliff had produced preliminary drawings for an administration building, library, auditorium, music building, art center, and corporation yard. These designs, which concentrated sculptural stone ornament around doors and windows, tended toward the formality of Beaux-Arts classicism, reminiscent of the Berkeley campus. In the proposed administration building, for example, a domed rotunda was placed at the center of arcaded wings. Only in the proposed library, with its stepped façade, and the partially realized art complex, with its accretive plan, were the elevations free of formal symmetry.

The art gallery/museum, opened in 1925, was the architect's first major work on the campus. Situated on a sloping site at the north edge of the campus, next to a streetcar stop, the building was intended as the first unit of a complex of galleries,

studios, and classrooms to be known as the Fine Arts Building. The gallery's two entrances had Renaissance/Baroque surrounds of carved stone, and a side porch was adorned with hand-carved capitals depicting famous artists.[40] The gallery space had a suspended ceiling of translucent glass. The building was enlarged several times according to the original design, notably by the 1933 addition of studios and an arcade composed of seven monumental arches, with the central arch framing the axial view to the south. The focal point of the complex, a domed tower encrusted with carved stone, was never completed.[41]

The Music Building, dedicated in April 1928 with a two-day concert festival, was Ratcliff's most fully realized project at Mills—a monumental design that came closest to embodying his vision for the campus, and his single most ambitious essay in Spanish Colonial Revival. The distinguished history of the music department that occupied the building, including the composer

Darius Milhaud and jazz pianist Dave Brubeck, has made it a landmark of cultural history as well, investing the architecture with the luster of life.

In the campus plan, the Music Building was intended to face an auditorium, an austerely elegant block set behind a broad parterre; accordingly, the original design was formally symmetrical: a high gable flanked by identical wings and elevated on a terrace. When the trustees decided instead to retain Lisser Hall, the old campus auditorium, Ratcliff relaxed the symmetry of the plan and elevation.[42] Though the building retained the central gable of the auditorium block—accentuated by a carved-stone entry with spiral columns, tympanum, and statuary—the studio and classroom wings to the sides had varied elevations and setbacks. An open porch ran the length of the east wing, terminating in a formal gable; the recessed

west wing ended in a casual grouping of gables and stairs. Cut into the base of Prospect Hill at the rear of the building was an amphitheater.

The interior was one of Ratcliff's most impressive. The foyer's arched ceiling was rendered in faux-wood plaster embossed with floral and vine-like motifs, and doorways were capped with carved-stone lintels of griffins and peacocks. The auditorium was adorned with stenciled beams, chandeliers of wrought iron, and frescoed murals depicting nudes in fauvist dreamscapes.[43] The feeling of spatial largesse was amplified by wide flights of stairs that led from the foyer to the balcony and upper corridors.

The other major campus project was a rambling dormitory complex set among pines atop Prospect Hill. It was built in three phases, beginning in 1926 with the Ethel Moore Residence Hall; an adjoining dormitory, Mary Morse Hall, was opened in 1935 and enlarged in 1944. The complex housed over two hundred dormitory rooms and a half-dozen living and dining rooms whose vaulted wood ceilings, fireplaces, and tall windows recalled Ratcliff's English halls. In finished form, the composite structure was the architect's largest work in the Spanish mode; its seven wings stepped up the hillside, ranging in height from one to four stories, enclosing patios and landscaped commons. The picturesque jumble of gables, balconies, stairways, and gated walls conveyed the feeling of a village that had grown over time.

Main entrance, Music Building, Mills College. Spare stucco surfaces punctuated by carved stone ornament are hallmarks of the Spanish Colonial Revival style.

Main entrance, Music Building, Mills College. The elaborate surround is a mixture of medieval, Renaissance, and Baroque elements.

Ratcliff's office completed a wide variety of other projects for the campus. Wetmore Gate (1925), the main entrance on Seminary Avenue, consisted of tall, lantern-topped piers with wrought-iron gates, adjoined by a lodge and circular fountain. Richards Gate (1933), on the west side of the campus, had similarly tall piers connected by curving walls.[44] The Norman Bridge Health Center (1930) occupied an elevated site near the campus gymnasium. The clinic was

*Auditorium, Music Building, Mills College. The richly ornamented
performance hall includes stenciled motifs and frescos.*

Norman Bridge Health Center, Mills College, Oakland, 1930.
The old main entrance is embellished with ceramic tile and
molded terra cotta

Walter H. Ratcliff, Jr., in the 1920s. Then in his forties, the architect-banker was at the height of his career.

loosely planned, with a freshness in its use of materials and detailing: exposed concrete walls that showed the patterns of the board forms, roughly stylized, cast stone columns set into round-arch windows, an arcaded solarium glazed with steel-sash casements.[45] Faculty Village, a group of nine single-family and duplex houses built in the late 1930s and early 1940s on a wooded site by the main entrance, presented the appearance of a small subdivision of the period. The firm's final campus project, the 1944 addition

to Mary Morse Hall, was completed a year after Aurelia Reinhardt retired. The new administration favored a more modernist approach to campus design, and Ratcliff's tenure as supervising architect ended.[46]

Walter Ratcliff's work at Mills College garnered widespread notice. At the 1929 biennial exhibition of the Northern California Chapter of the American Institute of Architects, the Mills College Music Building received the organization's highest award.[47] The college projects were also published in professional journals. The work was featured in the June 1932 issue of the *Architect and Engineer*—the last published retrospective (and cover story) of his career.[48]

IN 1927, when Walter H. Ratcliff moved across Center Street from the First National Bank Building, where he had leased office space since 1909, into the new Chamber of Commerce Building, the change of address signaled the scope of his achievement. Though he was still in his forties, and his independent practice was not yet in its twentieth year, he had already left an indelible architectural imprint on Berkeley. His work was also well represented in other cities of the Bay Area, including San Francisco, Oakland, Piedmont, Kensington, El Cerrito, Alameda, Belvedere, Mill Valley, San Mateo, and Palo Alto, as well as in several outlying cities: Santa Cruz, Carmel, Ukiah, Redding, and Yreka.

The onset of the Depression a scant two years later led the building industry, and the architects and bankers who served it, into dire straits. The Fidelity Guaranty Building and Loan

Scott Coy Haymond. This wedding portrait was taken in 1924, when the architect was 25, one year after he graduated from UC Berkeley and joined Ratcliff's staff.

Association, which had experienced a nearly thirty-fold increase of its assets in the 1920s, lost much of its value in the first two years of the Depression. For McFarland, who had never known failure, it was all too much. Ratcliff's son Peter, who was McFarland's godson, went to work for Fidelity in 1932, right out of high school. He retained vivid memories of McFarland's final days at Fidelity. "He called Dad in and he said, 'Walter, we're busted. I've lost everything.' He

had a nervous breakdown and never did come back. His world fell apart." The 62-year-old financier became a bedridden recluse at the family home on Prospect Street, where he lived with his widowed stepmother. Walter and Muriel visited them nearly every weekend; Peter sometimes came by to take them on drives. When McFarland died, in 1940, he was not yet 70.[49]

Ratcliff had taken over the management of the building and loan in 1933, and soon became its president. With the long hours he put in at the Fidelity Building, there was little time left for the architectural office four blocks up Shattuck Avenue in the Chamber of Commerce Building.[50] At its height in the 1920s, the office had employed as many as eight draftsmen; now there was one, Scott Coy Haymond, who had joined the firm right out of school and would end up spending most of his career—thirty years—in Ratcliff's employ. Raised in Pasadena, where his father owned a dry goods store, Haymond attended the UC School of Architecture, earning bachelor's (1921) and master's (1923) degrees. He married soon after going to work for Ratcliff. In 1925 Haymond and his wife moved into the house he designed for them, a half-timbered cottage in the Berkeley hills where they raised their two children.[51]

The firm would eke out a depleted existence in the 1930s with commissions from a handful of clients. The office stayed on at the Chamber of Commerce Building, though it moved down one floor, from Room 411 to Room 310, about the time Ratcliff took over at Fidelity. Scott Haymond ran the office alone. His daughter remembered

Downtown Berkeley in the 1940s, looking north on Shattuck Avenue. The Chamber of Commerce/American Trust Building, where Ratcliff's practice was located during the Depression and World War II, dominates the skyline.

visiting him there: entering the quiet foyer, Ratcliff's glassed-in partition empty, her father alone at work with pencil and paper at a table in the large drafting room.

Though there is no way of knowing for sure, it seems likely that Haymond served as the principal designer of the buildings that came out of the

Ratcliff office during the Depression, particularly after Walter Ratcliff took over the management of Fidelity. The firm's mainstay during these years was Mills College; major projects included the campus clinic, dormitories, and faculty housing. Ongoing contracts with the Berkeley Unified School District were also of importance, including seismic upgrades to existing facilities. There were a few commercial commissions in downtown

Berkeley, of which a service station survives, and a few campus-related jobs, notably the Sigma Kappa sorority house. Seminaries remained dependable if depleted clients. The firm's concluding work on Holy Hill was the William F. Badè Memorial Building, on which construction began in the spring of 1941; this understated rear addition at the Pacific School of Religion housed the museum, library, and offices of Badè's Palestine Institute. With few exceptions, such as the West Berkeley YMCA (1939), an essay in the stripped-down aesthetic of the streamlined Moderne, the firm's Depression-era work was revivalist in spirit.[52]

In the twelve years between the onset of the Depression and America's entry into World War II, the Ratcliff office designed no more than a dozen houses. Most were located in Berkeley or Oakland; most were in the Spanish Colonial Revival style; and most were modest in scale. The exception was the 1938 Orinda residence of the celebrated mining engineer Charles W. Merrill, which bore comparison in size and cost with the Breed and Blood mansions of earlier decades. On landscaped grounds covering over an acre, the house had a U-shaped plan and the understated stucco façades of Monterey Colonial Revival. The firm's last prewar house was the 1941 Gulick residence, designed for Ratcliff's niece, the daughter of William F. Badè, whose 1906 house in Berkeley's Southside had been one of the architect's first commissions.[53]

The office's output all but ceased during World War II, as building materials were rationed and non-war-related construction was curtailed. With the exception of a single project at Mills College—a dormitory addition—the office subsisted by converting single-family houses to apartments. Toward the end of the war, Walter Ratcliff and Scott Haymond closed the office in the Chamber of Commerce Building and set up shop in the small mezzanine of the Fidelity Building. Because there was so little room, drawings and files had to be thrown away. But the firm survived.

Meanwhile, Walter's oldest son, Robert, a graduate of the UC Berkeley School of Architecture, was living in Chicago with his wife and three young children, working for the Navy. He'd always thought that one day he'd join his father's firm. That day was about to arrive.

Four A New Beginning

OVER THE course of four decades, Walter Ratcliff had achieved prominence as a Bay Area architect, particularly in Berkeley where his work contributed to the character of the city's residential, commercial, and academic settings. He had also prospered as a real estate investor, developer, and banker, providing his family with economic security and standing.

Life was good on Roble Road. Walter and Muriel were devoted parents, and the children had a charmed upbringing. The oldest, Robert and Peter, found endless ways to amuse themselves. They built a shed in the backyard for their "museum" of rocks and bones; they designed and built a couple of canoes and a rowboat; they roller-skated down the middle of Tunnel Road (there were fewer cars in those years). The girls, Margaret and Muriel, also close in age, collaborated with their mother in her various projects.

Muriel Ratcliff was an active woman. "She was physically very strong and very much involved in family business," Robert recalled. "We always had projects, and she was always there. In the afternoons we mostly enjoyed ourselves, either riding horses, which we had—there were two of them at that time—or playing baseball, or doing something of that kind. On the weekends my mother always had something planned. She was just a marvelous entertainer." Muriel led the children on long walks up the electric railway grade to Grizzly Peak on Sunday afternoons and took them to Cottage Baths in Alameda, where they could swim in a pool or the bay. She also took them around in her pony-cart. "I used to claim we were one of the first two-car families in Berkeley," Robert said. "She drove us to school in her wagon, this four-wheeled cart pulled by a Hungarian pony."

Walter Ratcliff remained fit, a legacy of his

John Wickson Thomas house, Indian Rock Avenue, Berkeley, 1956.
Exemplifying the Bay Tradition, this wood and glass, open-plan
residence by Robert Ratcliff has its main living area on the upper
floor, with a window wall oriented to the bay view.

athletic youth, and he imparted his love of sports and the outdoors to his sons. The Berkeley Tennis Club was located at the bottom of the hill, by the Claremont Hotel, and on Sunday mornings he would give the boys lessons. During the summer, there were outings to Inverness, near Point Reyes, and backcountry trips in the Sierra. Walter and Muriel were skiers in the days before ski resorts, and they took the children on winter treks to the Sierra, alighting from the train in a snow shed in the middle of the night to check into a hotel at Donner Pass.[1] Walter and Muriel also liked to entertain, and there were frequent parties on Roble Road. Since they both enjoyed music, performances were staged in the big living room, with voice and piano recitals by their friends. Walter often played violin and sang at these events. It all made an impression on the children, particularly Robert, who loved music and had a fine voice, like his father.

As the children grew older, the house grew smaller, and in 1923 Walter enlarged the rear wing with a pair of bedrooms adjoined by a sort of dressing gallery—a long, narrow room where each child was provided with identical built-in shelves, drawers, and closets. The last of the five children, Walter, was born in 1926.

In the early years at Roble Road, the elder Ratcliffs came by often to visit, and the grandchildren spent time at their home on Euclid Avenue. When their house burned in the 1923 fire, they moved in with Walter and Muriel, an arrangement

Entry hall and staircase, Thomas house.

made possible by the fortuitous addition of the new bedroom wing. They later moved back to the Northside, taking rooms at Cloyne Court, a gracious apartment building that catered to university faculty.[2] Walter Henry Ratcliff died at Cloyne Court in 1925, at the age of 85.[3]

Around the time of his father's death, at the peak of his professional success, Walter Harris Ratcliff acquired a 381-acre ranch in Mendocino County, on California's isolated north coast near the town of Gualala. Once covered in redwoods, the land had been logged more than once but retained great beauty. Creek canyons cut through the slopes to the ocean, where cliffs rose above rock-fringed coves and beaches. The property, known as Sailrock Ranch, was gradually expanded to a thousand or so acres by acquiring adjacent parcels. It was a magnificent testament to the architect's love of nature.[4]

The family began spending summers on the ranch, and in the 1930s built a rustic retreat on the property. Walter's design incorporated a big stone fireplace and a broad veranda supported by unpeeled logs. The shingled house sat in a stand of young redwoods across the road from the shore, looking out to the sea.

FROM AN early age, Walter's oldest son showed an interest in architecture. "I used to walk in the hills with him, and we discussed how buildings were made," Robert remembered late in life. He would accompany his father to construction sites, learning about the proper way to mix plaster or lay a floor. By the time he was in high school, he knew he wanted to be an architect, unlike his

Robert and Evelyn Ratcliff cabin, Sailrock Ranch, Mendocino County, 1948 and later. Robert is seated at the piano in the central dining area.

two brothers, who would join Fidelity. He used to spend time at his father's office, getting to know the draftsmen, especially Scott Haymond.

Robert Ratcliff entered the University of California in 1932, graduating four years later with a B. A. in architecture. He was a member of the Alpha Delta Phi fraternity, whose big brick house at the top of Holy Hill was literally surrounded by his father's work: the Pacific School of Religion on one side, Church Divinity School of the Pacific on the other, University Christian Church right down the hill. Yet his father's brand of architecture no longer held interest for him: he wanted to be a modernist.

The university's School of Architecture, founded by John Galen Howard in 1903 and directed by him until his retirement in 1927, adhered to the methods of the Ecole des Beaux-Arts, with an emphasis on learning historical precedent and developing drawing skills. Following Howard's retirement, the school was headed by his protégé Warren Perry, and the faculty included Stafford Jory, Howard Moise, William C. Hays, Michael Goodman, Aram Torossian, and Raymond Jeans. When Robert enrolled there, a year after Howard's death, the old Beaux-Arts curriculum was very much in place, with required classes in drawing, painting, clay modeling, and the history of art and architecture. A typical assignment for entering students was to take measurements of some detail on a campus building and make an ink drawing based on the measurements.

Classes were held in a shingled building, known as the "Ark," at the north edge of the campus.[5] The department was small (less than a dozen students in Robert's graduating class) and the intimate scale of the Ark enhanced the sense of camaraderie.

Beaux-Arts pedagogy corseted the school, but modernism titillated the students. Exciting advances in Europe had trickled down to mainstream American design via the stylized abstractions of Art Deco and the streamlined forms of Moderne, but the students didn't want their modernism watered down, they wanted it straight.

"I can remember being very frustrated because on the outside we heard and read about Gropius and Breuer and Le Corbusier and Frank Lloyd Wright," Robert said of his student years. "And all these people were talking about contemporary architecture. Whereas on the inside the guys we were studying with were not. When we were seniors Warren Perry gave us a project: 'Design a palace in the manner of Peruzzi.' Peruzzi was a contemporary of Michelangelo! This was at the same time that the Bauhaus was going on, Mies van der Rohe!" Once he was out of school, Robert never looked back.

The modernism that captivated Robert Ratcliff was the stuff of dreams, a potent blend like the one that had enchanted his parents and their peers in Berkeley at the turn of the century. In its broadest, deepest sense, modernism was utopian rationalism of the sort that began to permeate Western society in the Renaissance and only reached the saturation point in the mid-twentieth century. Modernists believed in the power of the human intellect to understand, control, and ultimately reshape reality. This mindset resulted in highly organized nation-states that, however diverse ideologically, were united by their belief in scientific inquiry and technological progress as a paradigm for human advancement.

For architects, the modernist worldview involved a near-total reorientation—a turning away from historical inquiry to a more rational and utilitarian preoccupation. The shift in emphasis did not occur all at once, but gradually, over the course of several centuries. At the same time in American history that academic eclecticism became the dominant architectural paradigm, a mature modernist counter-paradigm began to emerge on the prairies around Chicago in the steel-frame skyscrapers of Louis Sullivan and the houses of Frank Lloyd Wright. These revolutionary buildings did not look to the past; rather, they confronted issues of form, function, space, and structure in a direct and "timeless" manner, seemingly without precedent, as if to remake the world afresh with each heroic act

The Ark, UC Berkeley, as it appeared soon after completion in 1906. The Arts and Crafts styling of the School of Architecture harmonized nicely with its Northside setting, which included nearby shingled houses on Hearst Avenue.

of creation: existential freedom made manifest in steel, stone, and wood.

The actual precedent for Wright's houses had been the Arts and Crafts movement, with its dual focus on nature and abstraction. The simplified vernacular forms and stylized open interiors of English Arts and Crafts houses had also influenced a whole generation of European architects, giving rise to a bewildering array of "new," "young," "free," and "breakaway" styles that flourished on the Continent between the 1890s and World War I.[6] The degree to which those diverse but related idioms embodied simplicity and abstraction was the measure of their contribution to an emergent modernism. In America, Wright achieved a synthesis of the archaic and progressive tendencies in the Arts and Crafts movement by fusing nature romanticism and abstraction into an integral whole. In him the movement can be said to have attained its fullest expression, reaching its end as an avenue of artistic exploration, and in him modernism began in earnest.[7]

The wholesale shift to conservatism in America after World War I eclipsed architectural modernism. Wright retreated into the shadowy recesses of a troglodytic expressionism. Yet in Europe, where the sense of postwar loss was infinitely greater, a flourishing avant-garde demonstrated that there was no point in resisting the new when the old had been annihilated. At the Bauhaus workers' collective, the German architects Walter Gropius, Marcel Breuer, and Mies van der Rohe purified the modernist paradigm, reducing it to its essential elements in the spirit of Mies's dictum "Less is more." In France, the Swiss-born painter and architect Le Corbusier moved toward a new architecture of mass-produced houses that would function as "machines for living."

So it was that architectural ideas engendered in England and America in the late nineteenth century reached their logical limit in Europe in the early twentieth, influencing in turn the next generation of architects in America. The middle third of the twentieth century was the zenith of modernism as an international lingua franca, characterized at its best by purity of form and clarity of structural and spatial expression. Modernists claimed moral superiority based on uncompromising integrity and honesty; historicist designers were dismissed as hopelessly retrograde, derivative poseurs mired in a dead past. Like the flappers who shed corsets, slips, and heavy muslin to reveal their bodies, avant-garde modernists unclothed their buildings, stripping away layers of eclectic appliqué to expose their form. Modernism, in a word, was sexy.

The new architecture found a receptive home in 1930s America, an era of profound social and economic change that belied the complacencies and denials of the 1920s. Coolidge's "The business of America is business" became Roosevelt's "The only thing we have to fear is fear itself." Under Roosevelt's New Deal, the radical intervention of the federal government into the nation's economic life became a daily reality—a rationalist subversion of received tradition that was at core a modernist enterprise. Federal (and federally funded) architecture of the period frequently conveyed this feeling of urgency, and a similar re-imagining characterized the culture at large. Set against the withdrawal and fantasy of the previous decade was the desire to confront and remold reality.

Architectural modernists believed they had the power and the vision to satisfy this desire, and the 1930s marked the reemergence of modernism in America. Gropius, Breuer, and Mies left Germany for the United States, fleeing fascism.[8] Gropius and Breuer taught at Harvard; Mies settled in Chicago. In 1932, the year Robert Ratcliff entered school, Philip Johnson and Henry-Russell Hitchcock curated the country's first exhibition of modern architecture at the Museum of Modern Art in New York, coining the phrase International Style. In 1936, the year Ratcliff graduated, Frank Lloyd Wright designed Falling Water, an iconic work that signaled the rebirth of his career. Modernism supplanted classicism as the new "international style," the sine qua non of the profession.

In California, modernism took root in different places in different ways. In boundary-less Los Angeles, the state's most populous urban area, where Frank Lloyd Wright's few postwar houses were concentrated, expatriate Austrian architects Rudolf Schindler and Richard Neutra designed buildings as advanced as any in Europe, making Los Angeles a center of progressive architecture in the 1920s.[9] Less-is-more modernism seeped into Bay Area architecture as an abstracted mood in certain revivalist buildings of the 1920s before assuming more overt form in the 1930s. The pioneer in this regard was William Wurster, a native Californian who graduated from Berkeley's School of Architecture in 1919; in his signature work, the Gregory farmhouse of 1927, he combined ranch-house revivalism with a subtle

Bernard Maybeck, the patriarch of Berkeley's Arts and Crafts tradition, and Robert Ratcliff several years before Maybeck's death, in 1957, at 95. Ratcliff was a child when he first met Maybeck.

abstraction of form and space.[10] Early Bay Area modernism, as seen in the houses of Wurster, Gardner Dailey, and their followers, would persist in its embrace of vernacular tradition and wood craftsmanship, evidence of an abiding Arts and Crafts sensibility; and it was this feeling of continuity, in designers as disparate as Maybeck and Wurster, that would give rise to the term "Bay Tradition" (and its variants) to connote a regional architecture.[11]

AT BERKELEY's School of Architecture, as at virtually every other school in the country in the 1930s, academic eclecticism remained the language of the professors. Their students had to learn the new idiom on their own. Robert Ratcliff was no exception. He became a modernist while attending classes taught by traditionalists. A year after his graduation, following a trip to Europe, Robert married Evelyn Trueblood Paine, who had

Graduating class at the Ark, UC Berkeley School of Architecture, 1936. Evelyn Paine has her coat draped over the forehead of Robert Ratcliff. Their classmate Worley Wong (second row, left) became a respected residential designer in the Bay Tradition in partnership with John Campbell (Campbell & Wong).

graduated with him in the 1936 class of the UC Berkeley School of Architecture. The wedding, in June 1937, took place near the campus, at St. Mark's Church, where Robert's aunts Mary and Ethel Ratcliff had been married earlier in the century. Evelyn, who soon became pregnant with their first child (Lucy, born in the spring of 1938), did not pursue her career.

Robert applied for work with numerous architects, including William Wurster and Gardner Dailey, but few buildings were going up in the waning years of the Depression. He found a job in the small Oakland office of Clarence Mayhew; when the work ran out, in 1937, he secured a position with the San Francisco firm of Masten & Hurd, whose partners had worked for his father at the outset of their careers. During his four years there, in a quickening economy, he worked on schools, commercial buildings, and residences, gaining in confidence and experience.

Robert and Evelyn were both children of the Berkeley hills, though from very different milieus. Claremont was a world away from Panoramic Hill, Evelyn's home, a south-of-campus enclave dotted with strange and stylish houses owned by artists and academics. A case in point was the Paine residence, perched on a steep lot on Panoramic Way; a post-and-beam box incongruously capped with a gently rounded roof, it had been designed and built in 1917 by her father, the sculptor Robert Paine.[12]

In 1941, the year Robert received his license, he and Evelyn moved into the house they had designed for themselves on Panoramic Way—a landmark of Bay Tradition modernism built with a $4,500 loan from Fidelity. Situated next door to the Paine residence, on land inherited from Evelyn's mother, the redwood structure occupied a tapering site wedged into one of the street's hairpin turns. Its shed roofs echoing the angle of the hillside, the house stepped up the slope on three levels. The main entrance was from the lower street, with a stairway ascending to the main living area, a living-dining room that looked out to the bay. Folding glass doors opened the room to a deck with railing of diagonal copper tubes. Copper skin was applied to the ceiling, and copper veneer encased the corner fireplace.

In an unpublished letter to the *Architectural Forum* (with plans and photographs) Ratcliff discussed the design:

> Considerable thought was expended on how to achieve a feeling of space with such a small actual floor area and no chance to expand in the horizontal dimension. The fact of its being on a hillside helped in this regard. In the living room, the ceiling, following the contour of the hill, rises from seven feet, six inches on the west to fourteen feet on the east. The deck beyond the glass west wall is seemingly incorporated in the living room space even when the folding glass doors are closed.

Space was harder to come by following the birth of their second child, Mary (Polly), in 1942. But such questions could be put off for a while; by 1943, the family was living in Chicago, where Robert spent the duration of the war as a civilian working in the engineering department of the central procurement agency of the Navy SeaBees, supervising mass-produced modular construction. The job, which appealed to his modernist sensibilities, gave him basic training in management skills and honed his leadership style (ask a lot of your team but keep it friendly). Robert and Evelyn liked Chicago. They frequented the museums and sought out buildings by Wright and Sullivan; Robert joined a choral group, and he took a class at the Illinois Institute of Technology, where he met Mies van der Rohe. Their third child, Christopher (Kit), was born in Evanston two weeks before Christmas in 1943.

Robert and Evelyn Ratcliff house, Panoramic Way, Berkeley, 1941. Partial view of the south elevation, showing the glass-enclosed stairwell to the study at the top of the main staircase.

ROBERT RATCLIFF joined his father's firm immediately after the war, flying home on a DC-3 a few days after VJ Day, in August 1945, leaving Evelyn and the children to follow later. He rushed back at his father's urgent request for assistance in the design of a dormitory complex in the hills south of campus—the firm's first major commission from the University of California. University officials were frantically preparing for the most intensive growth in the institution's seventy-seven-year history: a more than doubling of the enrollment at Berkeley, to over twenty-five thousand, and the new dormitories were needed immediately. The commission came to Walter Ratcliff through his friend Robert Sibley, president of the University of California Alumni Association. A fellow graduate of the Class of '03 and a director of the Fidelity Guaranty Building and Loan Association, Sibley had collaborated with Ratcliff on a housing study for the university shortly before the war.

Named for the Victorian estate it replaced, Fernwald occupied a sloping site in the Smyth Tract, at the upper end of Dwight Way along the south flank of Panoramic Hill. It was the university's largest residential complex: ten dormitories with shared common rooms and a central dining hall, providing accommodations for seven hundred women. Driven by parameters of economy, speed of construction, and availability of materials, the design resulted in an assemblage of long, two-story, stucco-clad blocks in a stepped and tightly packed arrangement with the stripped-down feeling of wartime housing—thin walls, flat roofs, replicated doorways and windows. Nevertheless, there were subtle touches that alleviated the uniformity. The gently battered walls anchored the heft of the blocks as they rose from the slope, and bands of casement windows under the eaves lightened the corners.[13]

The firm's largest commission in twenty years, Fernwald signaled the reemergence of the practice. In addition to putting the office on a sounder financial footing, with renewed confidence, the project reestablished a working relationship with the university. It also brought Robert into the fold, setting the stage for the firm's reinvention at mid-century. As the first frankly "modern" design to come out of the office, curtailed as it was by the project constraints, Fernwald presaged a radically redefined look for Ratcliff buildings. This change did not occur overnight; eight years would pass before the transformation was complete and the historicist sensibilities of the father gave way to the future-oriented vision of the son.

THE NEW partnership was known as Ratcliff, Haymond & Ratcliff, and in 1946, after Fernwald's completion, the office moved from its cramped quarters in the Fidelity Building to the nearby Lester Hink Building, two doors down, at the northeast corner of Shattuck and Durant Avenues—the firm's fourth location in downtown Berkeley.[14] This upper-floor space was also small (two rooms adjoined by a storeroom not much larger than a closet), but it met the needs of the practice during the years of gradual growth in the late 1940s and early 1950s. The firm's first female employee, Barbara Baird, an expert typist who also knew how to draw, was hired at this time.

It was a new beginning for the firm. At its peak in the 1920s, the office had taken on dozens of important projects for a wide range of clients; in the 1930s the output had slowed to a trickle, virtually drying up during the war. Now commissions began flowing in again, though by no means at the pre-Depression level. Most of this work was residential: in the late 1940s and early 1950s, houses accounted for at least three-fourths of the commissions—yet they amounted to no more than a third of the revenues. More substantial projects, notably Fernwald, as well as seminaries, churches, sororities, fraternities, and the occasional commercial or apartment building, were essential to keep the business growing. The firm remained centered in Berkeley, the site of three-fourths of its jobs through 1960. Most other projects were in Oakland, or elsewhere in the East Bay, and a handful of houses were commissioned in rapidly growing suburbs like Orinda, Lafayette, and Danville. In terms of output and scope, the post–World War II office closely resembled the pre–World War I practice.

The firm showed two very different faces to the world—one looking back to precedent, the other forward to pure possibility. Scott Haymond and Robert Ratcliff embodied the divergent views, with Walter Ratcliff acting the uneasy part of mediator between his oldest associate and oldest son. The arrangement, at least in the beginning, was to let Robert expend his modernist energies on residential projects while Haymond handled the larger jobs. Walter's connection with the firm, after more than a decade at the helm of Fidelity, remained tenuous; he cultivated clients but mostly spent his time managing the affairs of the bank, leaving Haymond in charge of the office. He was also getting on—he turned 65 in 1946—and starting to think about retirement. Scott Haymond had spent his entire professional life in the

employ of Walter Ratcliff—in 1948, his tenure totaled twenty-five years—running the office for much of that time as if it were his own. "He was accustomed to doing everything," Robert recalled. "Writing specifications, doing all the designs, doing all the supervision—doing the whole show. He was a very bright guy." In the early years of the partnership, coincident with the postwar boom in church attendance, Haymond worked on a number of church projects, including San Carlos Community Church (1946), Piedmont Community Church (1948), and Loper Chapel (1948) at the First Congregational Church of Berkeley (where he and his wife were members). The designs ranged from Spanish Colonial Revival at San Carlos and Piedmont to red-brick Georgian Colonial Revival in Berkeley.[15]

Meanwhile Robert designed houses. Of the more than one hundred residential projects that came through the office in the fifteen years after World War II—at least twenty in the late 1940s, fifty or so in the early 1950s, slightly fewer in the latter half of the decade—a good percentage were designed by young Ratcliff. Most of these houses were built high in the hills above Berkeley and Oakland. In the East Bay, where scant vacant land remained that was easily accessible, outlying upland districts became the new edge of the expanding urban core. The ubiquity of the automobile meant that families no longer needed to be close to streetcar or interurban lines. On these winding roads and steep lots, houses were built off the street, perched above or below it, accessible by driveways and only secondarily by stairs or pathways.

Walter Ratcliff boosted his son's fledgling efforts by approving home loans. "Most of the projects I was doing after the war needed funding, and [my clients] would go down to the Fidelity and ask for a loan," Robert recalled. "Several people in the company balked at some of the designs I gave them. They would say, 'This is a freak. If we fund this, we will fall on our face . . .' My father would say, 'It's okay,' and then they would do it."[16]

Robert's modern houses subscribed to the Bay Tradition, rooted in the area's half-century-old Arts and Crafts ethos. "On residential work I really preferred working in wood," he said. "I was very impressed by people like Maybeck and Gutterson." He liked to talk about a "fourth dimension" in architecture, consisting of "warmth and comfort and a sense of location, things that related to nature." His hero was Frank Lloyd Wright; though he admired the intellectual rigor of architects like Mies, Gropius, and Neutra, he did not respond deeply to their International Style aesthetic. "I felt that there was something personal missing, really, in the whole modern movement," he said. "Oversimplification seemed unnatural, an unnecessary discipline." Accordingly, the abstracted forms of his houses were softened by generous amounts of natural wood inside and out. Open plans were articulated by chimney masses and low partitions, with fireplaces (often quite large) providing focal points and beamed ceilings serving as unifying elements. Combined living-dining spaces were opened to the sunlight and views by window walls and glass doors leading to decks, patios, and gardens.

An early postwar house in the Berkeley hills, the 1947 Brezee residence, displayed many of the qualities that made Robert Ratcliff's work distinctive as well as threatening to the conservative loan officers at Fidelity. Frank Brezee wanted a house with no right angles or doors, except in bathrooms and closets; the architect complied with skewed walls and an open plan. The house stepped down the hillside on three levels, clad in redwood boards and battens inside and out. A wide deck oriented to the bay view wrapped around the window walls of the main level—a single space defined by a concrete fireplace with angled partitions separating the living/dining area from the kitchen. Open-tread stairs with handrails of copper tubing led up to a bedroom/studio with fireplace, adjoined by entry and garage.[17]

Two Berkeley houses from 1951 were more typical of Ratcliff's work, in their cubistic, boxlike massing. The Choate residence, on upper Panoramic Way, sat high above the street, facing west to the bay. The main living level, lined with floor-to-ceiling windows, was reached by a driveway curving up and around to the entry. The Culver residence, straddling an isolated ridge at the top of Panoramic Way, utilized modular wood construction with infill graphite panels. The entrance off the driveway passed informally through a kitchen alcove to a combined living and dining area with a fireplace and deck. A beamed tongue-and-groove ceiling enclosed these spaces. Stairs descended to three small bedrooms.[18]

The 1957 Foster residence was one of Ratcliff's mansions. Built on a steep view lot in the north Berkeley hills, the house enclosed more than four

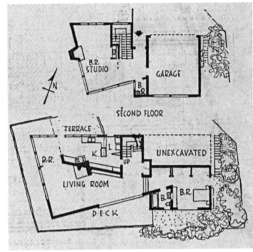

SECOND FLOOR

TOP LEFT: *Frank Brezee house, Shasta Road, Berkeley, 1947. The Berkeley hills were still relatively open when Rondal Partridge captured this image in the early 1950s.*
LEFT: *Angled walls, sloping ceiling, and glass doors opening onto an elevated deck contributed to the feeling of free-flowing space in the Brezee living room.*
ABOVE: *Brezee house, plan.*

FOLLOWING PAGES. LEFT: *A. M. Meads house, Roble Road, Berkeley, 1950. The balanced composition, banded windows, and extensive use of Roman brick make this one of Robert Ratcliff's most Wrightian designs.* RIGHT: *With its large fireplace and expansive windows framing a tangle of trees, the living room of the Meads house embodied the evolving Arts and Crafts experience.*

thousand square feet on its three levels, including a living/dining area adjoined by a study and cantilevered deck, three good-sized bedrooms with bathrooms, and a den. Though the house was more complex structurally, incorporating structural steel, it retained the rustic vocabulary of the architect's smaller houses. A patio garden with fireplace was nestled into the hillside by the glass-walled vestibule, providing a counterpoint to the endless space beyond the living room windows. This intimate garden was the work of Evelyn Ratcliff, who had become the landscape designer on many of her husband's residential projects.[19]

AMONG the firm's most important clients were seminaries, such as the Pacific School of Religion, Pacific Lutheran Theological Seminary, and Berkeley Baptist Divinity School (now American Baptist Seminary of the West). Shortly after the war, the Baptist seminary asked Ratcliff, Haymond & Ratcliff to prepare a master plan and initiate studies for several new buildings on the 28-year-old campus.

Founded in 1871, the seminary had come to Berkeley in 1904, three years after the Pacific Theological Seminary, taking up residence in the Southside. In 1919, the school moved into a new building at the corner of Dwight Way and Hillegass Avenue, four blocks south of the university campus. The four-story structure, a Tudor-Gothic composition in brick and terra cotta by Julia Morgan, stood across the street from the First Church of Christ, Scientist, Maybeck's 1910 eclectic masterpiece.[20]

The Ratcliff firm's chapel, library, and academic building (built between 1949 and 1954) shared a vocabulary reminiscent of the Church Divinity School of the Pacific. They harmonized nicely with Morgan's work: variegated brick sprinkled with dark clinkers and trimmed with stone; slate-covered roofs; mullioned windows; and buttressed porches with pointed-arch openings. Gothic arcades linked the chapel and academic building with the original building; the library formed an interior ell enclosing a landscaped green.[21] The ensemble achieved the sort of cloistered effect that had eluded Walter Ratcliff at the Pacific School of Religion.

The postwar persistence of historicism in the Ratcliff office, virtually unheard of at the time, was scandalous to born-again modernists who had long since repented of the sin of eclecticism. For Robert, a convert himself, it was cause for professional frustration and even embarrassment. His modernist convictions showed clearly in a building from the same period for a similar client: St. Margaret's House, the women's school on Holy Hill affiliated with the Church Divinity School of the Pacific. His father had designed a stucco-and-tile dormitory for the school in 1930, set back among trees at the corner of Hearst and Scenic Avenues, across from the university campus. Robert's 1952 chapel, one of his most affecting works, was lifted above the busy street on a high, battered base of buff-colored brick that fronted on the sidewalk and enclosed an oak-shaded courtyard at the rear. The wood-and-glass sanctuary,

George and Mary Foster house, San Luis Road, Berkeley, 1957.
View from living room past fireplace and hallway to patio garden.

not unlike an alpine cabin in its transparency and spreading gable, sat lightly on its elevated platform, an iconic symbol of Holy Hill itself.[22]

The contrast between Robert Ratcliff's modernist jewel and the equally polished works of his father and Scott Haymond could not have been more sharply etched; that they came out of the same office, at the same time, was remarkable. In effect, the firm was fluent in two languages as disparate in their syntax as Japanese and French. Each idiom encapsulated a different take on reality, a separate sense of beauty, and each had its own strengths and limitations. Had the firm continued to move in a direction that celebrated its bilingualism, a new synthesis might have emerged, one that could have enriched the region's architecture. But the opportunity was lost.

The modernist hegemony was still too jealous of its power and too zealous in its outreach to accommodate such heterodoxy. Robert himself could no longer abide a practice that he took to be hypocritical. The irony is that what he saw as sin later critics would see as salvation—an approach to design that was not two-faced but two-sided, its elements capable of being fused into a more nuanced language of contradiction and complexity.

As the Baptist work neared completion in 1953, the tensions within the firm reached the breaking point. The crisis was provoked by a project at the Pacific School of Religion: the campus chapel, a significant piece of Walter Ratcliff's scheme that had never been realized. Given his long association with the school, he assumed he would get the job; the trustees decided instead to conduct interviews.

The elder Ratcliff took it as a rejection, an implicit criticism of his work, and he declined the interview. Another, deeper problem was the fragmented design process within the office. Whereas Robert had produced preliminary drawings for a modernist building, Scott had done sketches for a Gothic Revival chapel along the lines of Walter's original concept. It was the St. Margaret's House/Baptist Divinity School disparity writ large, and neither side would budge.

FOR ROBERT, who had just turned 40, the issue went to the core of his professional credibility: "It would be a very prominent building, and I felt that my career was at stake." With his father's reluctant concurrence, he called a meeting at the office on a Saturday morning in the spring of 1953 and informed Scott Haymond that the partnership was no longer tenable. The severing of the cord was shockingly swift, considering all the man had done; so ended his thirty-year association with Walter Ratcliff and the Ratcliff firm. "Poor Scott really had a terrible time accepting it," Robert said late in life. "As a matter of fact, he never really got over the shock. It was too bad. I was sorry, but it had to happen."[23] Robert achieved what he had wanted since returning to Berkeley: a two-person partnership with his father. When the new name—Ratcliff & Ratcliff—was formally

PREVIOUS PAGES. LEFT: *Berkeley Baptist Divinity School Chapel, Hillegass Avenue, Berkeley, 1949. The diminutive English Gothic church was Walter Ratcliff's final design. Ratcliff, Slama & Cadwalader's 1964 addition to the seminary is partially visible on the right.* RIGHT: *St. Margaret's Chapel, Hearst Avenue, Berkeley, 1952. This small Episcopal church on the south flank of Holy Hill was Robert Ratcliff's first independent nonresidential commission.*

announced, he went to be interviewed for the Pacific School of Religion chapel, his first experience as lead on a major project:

> So with no political know-how, I talked to them about what I thought architecture was and what ought to happen in their chapel. I took along some examples of the kind of architecture that I thought was good architecture—not Gothic . . . They were not prepared for a contemporary approach. They were really thinking pseudo-Gothic like the rest of the campus. I got a lot of questions about this, and I ended up defending modern architecture. Anyway, I didn't get the job.[24]

The departure of Scott Haymond and his father's withdrawal left Robert the effective head of the partnership, and he began hiring architects who shared his modernist views. Murray Slama, a Bay Area native and recent Berkeley graduate, joined the firm in 1953, when he was around 30. Though inexperienced, he was a fast learner and soon became indispensable for his technical skills. "He could produce a set of biddable documents probably faster than anyone alive," remembered one colleague. Burns Cadwalader, hired in 1958, was primarily a designer. Slightly younger than Robert, he had grown up in small towns in California's Central Valley, learning to draft through correspondence courses; he had to drop out of Berkeley to support himself during the Depression but he persisted as an apprentice, eventually moving back to the Bay Area and obtaining his license when he was in his forties. Ratcliff would eventually make Slama and Cadwalader his partners, on very generous terms.

By the end of the 1950s, Robert Ratcliff was

Partridge house, Bear Creek, Contra Costa County, 1956; demolished. A Miesian box designed by Murray Slama in collaboration with the owner, photographer Rondal Partridge.

overseeing an expanding practice. Renovation work was beginning to come into the office from the University of California. There were numerous jobs for sororities and fraternities, reinforcing the firm's ties to the campus community, as well as commissions from the city government. Some of this work had a relaxed, suburban feeling, conveyed by broad, low-pitched gables and expanses of glass in wood and brick walls. The Northside's Live Oak Park Center (1957), with its attached auditorium, resembled a school from the suburbs. Alpha Epsilon Phi (1958), a large sorority on a prominent corner, brought the idiom to Piedmont Avenue's "Fraternity Row."[25]

Berkeley Fire Station No. 4, designed in 1959, was a public commission that responded sensitively to neighborhood concerns over the constricted, tree-covered site, which had long served as an informal park in Northbrae. A building-in-the-round, the station preserved more trees than a conventional plan would have allowed, and its pavilion-like form, encompassed by columns, paid homage to the site. It became an instant classic: one of the firm's best-known works of the decade.[26]

THE NAME Ratcliff & Ratcliff had by then become a fiction; a professional partnership between father and son had not existed for years. Walter began disengaging from active architectural work during the Baptist seminary project; the chapel, on which construction began in 1949, would be his last design. "He worked hard on the chapel," Robert recalled. "After that, he didn't spend very much time in the office." Walter had no heart for the modernist enterprise; it wasn't his way. And he was getting old. In 1951, he told Robert he would no longer draw a paycheck. The 1953 imbroglio over the PSR chapel, and Haymond's departure, marked the end of his career. He ceded control of the practice to his son, formally retiring in 1955 at age 74.

Robert proceeded to move the office around the corner to the Odd Fellows Temple, at Fulton Street and Bancroft Way, facing Edwards Stadium at the west edge of the campus—the firm's fifth and final location in downtown Berkeley. For the first time, the office was not on Shattuck Avenue; for the first time since the 1920s, it was not in a building designed by his father. The new location spoke to the 42-year-old son's professional arrival after a journey of twenty years.

Two projects from 1957 declared Robert's independence. The Holbrook Library Addition at the

Pacific School of Religion was a vindication of sorts, institutional atonement for the chapel debacle. The three-story addition was discreetly sited behind and down-slope from his father's Tudor-Gothic library and administration building. The vertical thrust of the molded concrete walls and windows was a modernist trope on Gothic energy, allusive rather than literal, and remarkably harmonious with the historicist landmark it adjoined.

The second project, near the Hillside Club, was a new church adjoining a half-timbered parish hall designed by the father in 1924. Like the Holbrook addition, All Souls Episcopal Church was stark in its modernity: exposed concrete and an abstract gable enclosing space. On the rear west wall of the complex, the gables of the parish hall and the church sat side by side, the old façade balanced and calm, the new one a hard-edged exercise in asymmetric assertion. Yet the roofs were interwoven in a way that was almost gentle, and the contrast of elevations was more dialogue than assault. Though the son spoke a different language, he remained courteous; he was not afraid to speak his mind, but he did so with respect.

Fire Station No. 4, The Alameda, Berkeley, 1960. Jules Kliot, a young designer new to the firm, proposed a circular building for the triangular site in order to preserve a stand of redwoods. The building expressed its Arts and Crafts romanticism in modern guise, including concrete columns evocative of tree trunks.

Five   Ratcliff, Slama & Cadwalader

THROUGHOUT the 1940s and 1950s, Robert Ratcliff had worked under the shadow of his father's legacy. Though the son's buildings clearly came from a different mold, most projects in those years remained centered in Berkeley, and commissions either replicated the kinds of jobs Walter Ratcliff was already known for, such as residences and churches, or they built on work for previous clients.

In the 1950s, following his father's retirement, Robert succeeded in remaking the office in a modernist mode. Yet it was only in the 1960s, when Ratcliff & Ratcliff gave way to a new partnership, Ratcliff, Slama & Cadwalader, that he could be said to have forged his own professional identity. Projects undertaken over the next two decades were more substantial and diverse, and they were dispersed over a much wider area. In this the firm was a product of its age—a player in a drama of metropolitan growth that imposed a new urban order on the cities and farmlands of the San Francisco Bay Area.

IT IS DIFFICULT to overstate to what degree the forces of modernity unleashed by World War II had reshaped the Bay Area. The global race for scientific, technological, and military supremacy had mobilized entire populations under centralized powers. In the United States, the federal government spawned research and development through fiat and funding, leading to significant advances in areas as diverse as systems management, modular construction, nuclear physics, and medicine. As a nexus in what President Eisenhower later termed the "military-industrial complex," the Bay Area drew hundreds of thousands of new residents to its factories, shipyards, and military facilities, setting

Lake Anza bathhouses, Tilden Park, Berkeley, 1965. Cadwalader's ensemble of wood pavilions sits lightly on its lakeside site.

the stage for the intensive urbanization of the postwar period.

The astonishing speed and scope of urban development in the quarter-century after the war attested to the competency of a technocratic culture equipped with powerful new tools, and with vast wealth at its command. America attempted to live out the modernist dream of remolding a messy and bewildering world into a rationally planned utopia. Modern architecture was both the reflection of this culture and its affirmation, a machined aesthetic that was functional, flexible, and porous to new technologies, the future-oriented vehicle of its heroic quest.

In the Bay Area, as elsewhere in America, federal dollars underwrote the creation of the new metropolis. Federally funded highways radiated out from the cities, the arteries of a spreading suburban corpus on a scale never before seen. The allure of the new—new subdivisions enabled by federal home loans, new schools subsidized by federal grants—acted like a vacuum sucking white families from the inner cities into sanitized environments devoid of decay or racial heterogeneity. The Bay Area's population doubled in the twenty-five years after the war, but Oakland and San Francisco actually lost residents during this same period; whereas before the war the two cities accounted for over half the Bay Area's population, by 1970 they accounted for less than a fourth.[1]

The environmental cost was as large as the undertaking. Tidelands were filled in; pastoral settings were plowed under. Fragile urban ecologies were also lost as widespread demolition destroyed decades-old harmonies of streetscape,

townscape, and city. This is not to say that California had not been subjected to similar forces in the past; indeed, the state's economic history since the gold rush was largely a chronicle of mining, logging, and farming, an epic tale of such wealth and natural devastation as to astonish the world. What was new was the urgent metropolitan impulse: the shift in focus from extraction and cultivation to urban development.

Berkeley was a microcosm of change in the region's older urban core. During the war the city grew by 40 percent, gaining thirty thousand residents in five years. Many were civilian workers who found employment in local factories as well as the nearby Kaiser shipyards in Richmond; they found shelter in hastily built apartments. After the war the city lost families to the suburbs, but it also attracted many new residents and students; as a result its wartime population base of 115,000 would hold steady.

The threads of history lingered in Berkeley's primarily residential urban fabric into the 1950s. In a patchwork of incremental growth, remnants of the nineteenth-century town lay scattered about; districts of Arts and Crafts houses fanned out from the university campus; tracts of bungalows and revivalist cottages blanketed the flatlands; and residences in many styles covered the slopes. The first waves of modernism had already swept through the city to crest high in the hills, leaving in their wake delicate stands of wood and glass. What unified this heterogeneous mass of buildings were resonant harmonies of scale: in neighborhoods, houses of similar size and placement; downtown, a consolidated whole.

The locus of new development was the University of California, which had long since outgrown its nineteenth-century campus. Expansion into the adjoining hills and neighborhoods had begun as early as the 1920s—notably Memorial Stadium (1923), whose environmental cost had been the destruction of pristine Strawberry Canyon, and Edwards Stadium (1932), built on the site of a historic Southside neighborhood. On the campus itself, the mood of Beaux-Arts coherence and classicism prevailed into the early postwar period, when most new buildings were still being designed to fit in with the historicist ensemble created by John Galen Howard and his successors.

All of this began to change in the 1950s, under the pressure of increased enrollment and with the hubris of an institution that had outgrown not only its physical setting but its identity as a state university. Berkeley scientists had helped create the atomic bomb, after all, and the campus, with its pantheon of Nobel laureates, now seemed to belong more to the world than to the city at its gates. So it was that the buildings that began to rise on the campus bore little if any relation to what preceded them; their physical setting had become, in a very real sense, irrelevant. Those towered offices, classrooms, libraries, and laboratories responded to a higher calling and a more abstract context: to fulfill the destiny of a great university on the world stage. Their enhanced size reflected the heroic scale of the enterprise as well as the sober realities of existence in a mass society, and their spare design embodied the pragmatic and forward-looking spirit of the culture that built them. Conceived from the inside out as functional envelopes for human activity, they mimed the haughty striptease of modernism in the certainty that what is exposed is truer than what is hidden.

And as the campus was irrevocably changed, as altered as the famous skyline across the bay, bristling with gleaming shafts of corporate power, the neighborhoods around the university were transformed by big-box apartment buildings, block-sized residential compounds, and high-rise dormitories.

The divinization of human progress envisioned by Berkeley's brown-shingle sages at the dawn of the twentieth century had indeed become historical reality, at least as ideology, though in ways those more innocent prophets could not have imagined. When the Ratcliffs first moved to the university town—when land was plentiful and people were not—they had been able to participate in the creation of a community unfettered by tradition and submissive to nature. By the 1960s, when electric anthems of self-actualization reverberated through the culture, the region pulsed with an urban energy appropriate to mass society. The towers that rose from the teeming campus and crowded neighborhoods were nothing less than the fulfillment of prophecy.

BY THE time Ratcliff, Slama & Cadwalader was established, in 1961, creative control had long since passed from the retired founder to his son.[2] Robert, who turned 48 that year, was in his prime, and his new partners were men he had hired and groomed, fellow modernists who shared his vision of the world.

The three architects made a stable triumvirate.

Murray Slama's emphasis on cost-effective productivity served as a check and balance to Burns Cadwalader's more idealized focus on design, and both men worked well with the firm's second-generation scion. The partners were energized and engaged by the urban élan of the era, but under Ratcliff's guidance the practice remained rooted in its Berkeley-bred ethos of community and nature: client service (and staff solidarity) wedded to the woodsy regionalism of the Bay Tradition. The tension between urban realism and nature-oriented romanticism would remain a defining, and poignant, feature of the firm during the partnership's seventeen-year existence— indeed, to the present day.[3]

In 1962, the office moved out of its warren of rented rooms in the Odd Fellows Temple to a renovated warehouse at Adeline Street and Grove Street (now Martin Luther King, Jr., Way), a mile and a half to the south. Prominently sited on the Berkeley-Oakland border at the confluence of two crosstown thoroughfares, the new quarters provided ample room for the growing practice.[4] For the first time since its inception, the Ratcliff office was no longer located in downtown Berkeley. The move symbolized the renewed, regional stature of the firm. As commissions grew in size and complexity, the office staff expanded from under a dozen to nearly thirty individuals.

Within the partnership, Robert Ratcliff found himself doing less actual design work and project management as he took on the roles of cultivator of commissions and father figure to the staff. He was the public face of the firm, the principal who made initial contact with clients and presentations at interviews. He performed these duties with the ease of a natural mixer and a sense of entitlement. As a lifelong resident of Berkeley and an alumnus of the university, Ratcliff seemed to know everyone. He devoted generous amounts of time to community causes, serving on the boards of the Berkeley Municipal League, Council of Social Planning, Berkeley YMCA and YWCA, and the Berkeley Community Concerts Association, and he regularly attended meetings of the City Commons Club and Rotary Club. As an activist and conservationist, he was a leader in the fight to stop a mammoth development that would have doubled Berkeley's land area by adding fill to the bay, creating a new city on the municipal tidelands.

His partners were also active in civic and professional groups, not least the East Bay Chapter of the American Institute of Architects (AIA), where they both served terms as president. Through their contacts, they were able to bring in work, especially Cadwalader, an Oakland resident who secured school and park commissions through his involvement in service organizations such as the Oakland Public Schools Citizens' Committee, Oakland Citizens Committee for Urban Renewal, Oakland Design Advocates, and People for Open Space.

Ratcliff paid close attention to the office morale. "The only assets in an architectural firm are the people," he was fond of saying. Asked what particular talent he brought to the table, he would quip, "Keeping everybody happy." He felt that he was "good at getting good people and keeping them working together well: recognizing their ability and somehow encouraging them." The firm became known for its "family" ethos (not standard practice in the profession), with a high degree of employee loyalty, low rates of turnover, and many returnees, often after years of absence.

As WORK ballooned, projects continued to employ the modernist approach to planning and design first articulated by Robert Ratcliff in the 1940s and 1950s. The sober-minded modernism practiced by the firm in the 1960s and 1970s, restrained and tasteful, was tailored to fit the requirements of the client, and it was proffered in a spirit of social responsibility. Design decisions, in other words, were primarily responsive to the people who would be most directly affected by them—and whose needs Ratcliff, in particular, was expert at eliciting—rather than the opinions of peers or the desire to be published.

Design was also a product of the office's inclusive culture. The partners approached the process as a collaborative effort: "Everyone can design" became an office byword. This method, excellent as it was for morale and training, could result in buildings that were clearly articulated but lacked the timbre of an individual voice. Ratcliff himself felt that neither he nor his partners "were really original thinkers, inventing new ways, on the cutting edge." More than he realized, he remained his father's son: the "Ratcliff" brand of modernism of the 1960s and 1970s was analogous to the "Ratcliff" historicism of the 1910s and 1920s: highly competent, generally conservative, and committed to client needs.

Of the three partners, Burns Cadwalader seemed to respond most deeply to design as a calling. He imbibed his modernism at a variety of sources, apprenticing in Redding under Clayton Katz, a protégé of Ernest Kump, and later working for the Richmond firm of Hardison & Komatsu, whose partners had close ties with the noted modernist Vernon DeMars. In his own work, Cadwalader combined Katz's functionalist minimalism with an expressive formalism derived from Wright, and with Ratcliff he shared a partiality to the region's lingering Arts and Crafts aesthetic within the Bay Tradition.

Murray Slama occupied a special niche in the office; in a sense, he was to Robert what Scott Haymond had been to Walter—an utterly competent and dependable right-hand man who could handle just about anything. "Murray was an interesting guy," Robert remembered. "He felt that a building wasn't finished until it was built. I found him very valuable in many ways—not so much from a design point of view as from his ability to organize his work, his practical knowledge, and his ability to think things through. I felt very confident, when he had done something, that it would work, that there wasn't some hard decision he had avoided." Slama spent most of his career—twenty-five years—with Ratcliff. In his prime, he was a turbocharged, chain-smoking super-professional who embodied the technocratic energy of his age. He gave countless hours to the AIA and also found time to write the *Construction Inspection Manual* (1973), a classic of its genre that would go through six editions and become a standard text in schools, offices, and government agencies.[5]

Three architects who began their long association with the firm in the 1960s were Peter Scott,

Co-op Shopping Center, El Cerrito, 1963.

Don Kasamoto, and Sy Husain. Scott, a Stanford-trained designer, and Kasamoto, a Hilo-born graduate of Berkeley, were both in their late twenties when they were hired in 1962. "I was the first non-UCB architect to enter the firm and play a role that was significant," Scott recalled. "I introduced Bob/Burns/Murray to a wider sensibility, among other things to the possibility of hiring from other sources. Designwise, the firm grew in sophistication as a result."[6] Kasamoto developed into a versatile manager who worked well with

people and oversaw numerous projects. The older Husain, a native of India and also a Berkeley graduate, would begin working with the firm as a collaborator on a large health care project and stay on to establish its successful practice in this area.

THE 1960s were a heady time for the young partnership. As the arc of development spread outward from the Bay Area's population centers to the hinterlands, work inundated the office to an extent not seen since the 1920s. The firm moved beyond its traditional client base in Berkeley and

Oakland to take on an array of projects east of the hills, in rapidly growing suburban cities like Livermore, San Ramon, Danville, Walnut Creek, Concord, and Brentwood. The burgeoning academic and health care segments of the practice expanded operations south to Monterey Bay, east to the Central Valley, and north toward the Oregon border. Within the confines of the metropolitan Bay Area, however, Ratcliff, Slama & Cadwalader remained closely linked to the East Bay and its phalanx of suburbs, doing little work in San Francisco, Marin County, the Peninsula, or the South Bay.[7]

The firm's principal commission at the outset of the sixties, begun in tandem with the partnership, was the Co-op Shopping Center in El Cerrito,

next door to Berkeley. The design, one of the office's most inventive from this period, consisted of a cluster of hexagonal wood pavilions with tent-like roofs whose laminated beams left the vaulted interiors open. Completed in 1963, the project was a high-minded attempt to turn a generic building type into a distinctive environment: the village-like setting and expressive rusticity of the forms provided a vivid contrast to typical malls.[8]

If the Co-op Shopping Center represented Ratcliff, Slama & Cadwalader at its most "Berkeley"—romantic idealists jousting with urban realities—the largest commissions to come through the office in the 1960s were exercises in cultural accommodation. Technically and programmatically demanding, these projects in Oakland for the county government required assistance from firms with specialized skills. The Alameda County Administration Building and

Alameda County Administration Building, Oakland, 1964. Designed in collaboration with Van Bourg Nakamura, this project inaugurated the Ratcliff practice of partnering with other firms.

Alameda County Parking Structure, Oakland, 1964. A modernist landmark in the county government complex, with Van Bourg Nakamura.

Parking Structure (1964) was designed in association with Van Bourg Nakamura, an Oakland firm with a hefty portfolio of city halls and courthouses.[9] The commission came about in part through Ratcliff's political connections—he knew the chairman of the county's board of supervisors, a former member of the Berkeley city council— but it owed as much to the partners' determination to become players on the high-stakes field of institutional growth. Winning the contract in competition with Warnecke & Warnecke, a nationally known firm, was a coup.

The program called for a building to house eleven courtrooms, the offices of the board of supervisors, and other county offices, together with a separate parking structure, on adjoining block-sized parcels across from the old courthouse—a Moderne high-rise on Lake Merritt erected in the 1930s for a jurisdiction whose population had now nearly doubled.[10] Van Bourg Nakamura took primary responsibility for design; Ratcliff served as "executive architect," handling all aspects of project management. The inside-out, functionalist planning of the administration building resulted in a four-story structure with an exposed concrete cage and infill of aggregate panels slit by narrow windows. Like contemporary buildings on the Berkeley campus, it served its purpose but ignored its setting. More successful as a stand-alone design was the parking structure, the largest in Oakland, an eight-story, cylindrical stack that stood as a classic example of engineering logic applied to the problem of automotive glut.[11]

This high-profile job taught the firm a lesson it never forgot about the effectiveness of collaborative ventures on large projects. It also brought the office into close contact with county officials. The experience bore fruit when the firm won its second big commission from Alameda County, in 1964, for an addition to Highland Hospital, in East Oakland.[12] As had been the case with the courthouse and parking structure, the office had no experience in health care design. The collaborator on this project was Rex Whitaker Allen, a San Francisco practice that had carved out a niche in health care architecture. Several members of Allen's staff were loaned to the Ratcliff office for the duration of the project, including the lead architect, Jan Smeckens, and his assistant Syed (Sy) Husain.

Highland Hospital, Oakland, 1969. Designed with Rex Whitaker Allen, this 363-bed replacement hospital for Alameda County's acute care facility launched Ratcliff's modern health care practice.

Highland Hospital had been built in the 1920s from the design of Henry H. Meyers, the county's official architect. The rambling Spanish Colonial Revival complex had wings projecting from a circulation core; rows of windows gave the wards maximum exposure to sunlight and air, considered at the time to be essential curative agents. Since World War II, scientific advances in medicine, in particular antibiotics and other drugs, had revolutionized the treatment and prevention of disease. Modern medicine, like higher education, presented irrefutable evidence of the efficacy of postwar technocratic culture. Modern hospitals, like their sibling towers on college campuses, encoded their high calling in the aesthetic of functionalism.

Ratcliff and Allen's addition fit this modernist model. A seven-story steel-and-concrete slab with curving façade and narrow ranks of fixed windows, it made no gesture to the existing hospital campus; its scale and context were metropolitan. If the 1920s hospital was essentially a shelter for sick people, a handsome and humane but ultimately ineffectual environment that looked outward to nature for solace, the 1960s facility was its opposite—a laboratory for healing, abstract and cerebral, that looked inward to a cleansed environment inhabited by white-smocked technicians tending arcane instruments, performing delicate operations, and disbursing from a wondrous pharmacopoeia. If it can be said that modern health care pronounced judgment on traditional medicine, then its architecture, through association, helped supplant traditional design. Modern medicine legitimized modern architecture, and hospitals would remain exemplars of functionalism on an institutional scale.

Syed Husain stayed on after Highland was finished. Born in Hyderabad, India, he had come to the Unites States in 1949, when he was 22, to pursue an architectural education; his studies in India had been interrupted by the political turmoil of independence. Accepted by Columbia, Pratt, and Berkeley, he chose Berkeley—now a modernist school, under the tutelage of William Wurster, Joseph Esherick, and others—where he lived at the International House, worked as a waiter, and finally graduated with a B.A. in 1955. His interest in health care, sparked by a job designing nursing homes, had led him to Allen and then to Ratcliff.

It would become Husain's burden over the course of his thirty-five-year career at Ratcliff to find a balance between the technical needs of health care and the human needs of its patients.

His perspective, which he characterized as a "holistic, patient-centered approach," required an understanding of the patient's experience. Among his innovations was the hiring of doctors and nurses as full-time staff to work with the firm's architects on projects. He also led planning forums for hospital administrators and health care professionals. Husain assiduously cultivated clients, bringing in a steady flow of projects in the Bay Area and beyond: as far south as the Salinas Valley Memorial Hospital by Monterey Bay, as far east as the Modesto City Hospital in the Central Valley. He found a champion for this work in Murray Slama. The two made an effective marketing team, and Slama was principal in charge on Salinas, Modesto, and other health care projects. Modesto, a low-rise addition completed in 1978 for $3 million, was a representative design of the period; the minimalist concrete shell, with canopies for shade, belied the complexity of the program.[13] Projects like this would be dwarfed in the 1980s by facilities for major health care providers.

RATCLIFF, Slama & Cadwalader took on dozens of other projects in the 1960s and 1970s, in a diverse practice ranging from the older East Bay cities to the suburbs and more distant locales in northern California. The firm's suburban commissions were among its most memorable work from these years.

Livermore, home to the UC-administered Lawrence Livermore Laboratory and one of the region's fastest growing suburbs, commissioned a master plan for a new civic center. The multistory Police and City Administration Building, the

Library, Athenian School, Danville, 1970. Now known as the Eleanor Holt Dase Center for the Arts, the hillside building incorporated large wood-sash windows and a balcony overlooking the creek.

centerpiece of the group, was sited on a low rise, fortresslike, its angular concrete walls and exposed truss-work declaring the urban aspirations of the client. In a civic center plan for a smaller city, Brentwood, the firm devised a more casual grouping of hipped and shed-roofed pavilions on manicured grounds, similar to the hexagonal pods of Los Cerros Elementary School, near Danville.

Park and recreation buildings often incorporated a rustic aesthetic to sustain the illusion of close-to-nature existence in urbanizing environments. Elaborate wood appliqué around the upper-story windows of the Concord Recreation Center softened the massing of its brick forms.

The Las Positas Golf Course clubhouse employed an all-wood palette; yet it was sited next to Livermore's municipal airport, and the roof, a dramatic cantilever with upswept prow, paid homage to the technological wonder of flight.

For private clients as well, Ratcliff, Slama & Cadwalader seemed intent on exporting the seasoned urban romanticism of the Bay Tradition to raw suburban settings. Pleasant Hill's Church of the Resurrection, a small building with a big budget, was notable for the bell-curve vault of its wood-paneled sanctuary, formed of free-span laminated beams reminiscent of Maybeck's Hearst Hall.

The Athenian School, on seventy-five acres of oak-studded grassland in the foothills east of Danville, allowed the firm to express its Arts and

Crafts sensibilities on the scale of a small campus. The master plan grouped the principal buildings around a giant valley oak at the lower end of the grounds; other buildings bordered a pair of streams, leaving a wide sloping meadow at the center. In one of his last solo efforts, Ratcliff designed the main building, Kate and Dyke Brown Hall (1965), in a chalet-like idiom of broad gables and glass that recalled his 1952 chapel for St. Margaret's House.[14]

Among the beneficiaries of suburban growth were recreational facilities in the outlying regions. Sierra ski resorts, glamorized by the 1960 Winter Olympics at Squaw Valley, did a booming business. For Bear Valley, a new resort south of Lake Tahoe, the firm devised a general plan as well the main lodge and condominiums, rendered in the shingled, sharp-edged style of alpine modernism.

In the older cities of the East Bay, notably Oakland, the office continued to take jobs for public agencies, often in a climate of racial tension and economic disparity that contrasted with the blithe, monocultural expansionism of the suburbs. Under federal guidelines for Great Society agencies like the Department of Housing and Urban Development (HUD), regulatory issues were complexified and communitarian ideals codified in the ritualized input of public hearings and workshops. The firm's principal monuments to that time and place were Stonehurst Elementary School (1975), in East Oakland, and the West Oakland Multi-Service Center (1977), a facility that included

Church of the Resurrection, Pleasant Hill, 1961. A lavishly layered wood aesthetic applied to a modern suburban sanctuary.

a branch library. The formal expressionism and spatial drama of these projects, designed by an emerging talent, Crodd Chin, also bore the imprint of Cadwalader, who submitted to the rounds of public meetings with cheerful resolve. In the island city of Alameda, adjoining Oakland, Chin worked with Kasamoto on the city's Police Administration Building (1978), a streamlined structure that was given a red-brick veneer to harmonize with the adjacent 1890s City Hall.

Corporate/institutional clients like the Bank of America, American Automobile Association, and the state's utility giant, Pacific Gas & Electric (PG&E), were another important source of work. The firm designed branches for the Bank of America in the Central Valley towns of Atwater and Blossom Hill, and in Oakland. These buildings had a security-conscious formalism, combining tilt-up concrete and brick massing with spare fenestration and a regard for fine detailing. The Bank of America's Oakland main office (1979), a prominently sited downtown building, was a collaboration with the San Francisco office of HOK, an international firm with numerous corporate clients.

Peter Scott's designs for the Berkeley and Oakland offices of the California State Automobile Association (AAA) revealed his concerns for color and texture. The Berkeley office was clad in tan adobe brick capped by green copper, enclosing a wood-paneled vaulted interior. The Oakland office, a showcase of masonry construction, utilized fine sand-mold brick throughout. The finished effect, with brick paving curving up to meet brick walls, suggested that the structure

*Pacific Gas & Electric Company, Engineering Research Center, San Ramon, 1967.
Dominated by its geodesic dome, the building housed mechanical and electrical
laboratories that could be reconfigured to meet changing technical requirements.*

varied from the soft gray of smoothly enameled
panels to the deep brown, sandpapery rust of
Cor-Ten steel.

Ratcliff, Slama & Cadwalader also revived the
academic element of the firm's practice. Since the
last project at Mills College, during World War II,
the Ratcliff office had not taken on such commissions outside of Berkeley. In the 1970s, the office
began a long association with the University of
the Pacific (UOP), in the Central Valley city
of Stockton. This was another of those jobs that
came about largely through Robert Ratcliff's
presentation skills; at the first interview he established a rapport with the school's president, Dr.
Robert E. Burns, leading to commissions for a
campus master plan, health center, student center,
music building, and science center, in addition to
several projects for the UOP Dental School in
San Francisco. The most notable of these was the
gabled, brick-clad student center on the Stockton
campus, housing a mix of uses in a multistory,
balconied building wrapping around a courtyard.

The firm was awarded commissions on other
campuses of the University of California for the
first time, including a radiobiology laboratory at
UC San Francisco and the student apartment
complex, child care center, and chancellor's
residence at UC Santa Cruz—the latter two
designed in the rustic Bay Tradition mode.[16]
Yet it was to UC Berkeley that the firm turned

emerged organically from its site, coalescing
within an unbroken membrane of materials.[15]

Working with designers Crodd Chin and Chuck
Trevisan, Scott oversaw the San Ramon Engineering Research Center, commissioned by Pacific Gas
& Electric. The job required a high level of technical understanding, which was reflected in the final
design. Built near the freeway at the edge of a
rapidly growing suburb, with sharply angular wings
and a geodesic dome—one of the largest in California—the futuristic structure exuded high-tech
brio. Color and texture on the all-metal cladding

*California State Automobile Association, Oakland, 1967. Working
under Murray Slama as principal in charge, Peter Scott approached
the project as a self-described exercise in "brickiness"—letting the
baked clay material emerge naturally from the site.*

most often for academic work, and Berkeley itself remained a constant in the company's evolving character.

BERKELEY was the fixed point that provided Ratcliff, Slama & Cadwalader with a historical identity. The firm took on projects throughout the city, from the flatlands to the hills, on campus and off. Its fifty-year association with the municipal government resulted in commissions for schools, libraries, and park buildings, and four decades of on-and-off dealings with the university finally produced a solid run of campus projects and student housing.

The firm's distinguished residential practice, a Ratcliff tradition spanning seven decades, ended in the 1960s as the office produced its last designs for houses in the Berkeley hills. With the shift to larger, more profitable projects, there was neither time nor inclination to take on small jobs. External factors also played a role. Following decades of development, the hills retained few buildable sites, let alone view lots, that didn't require extensive engineering. There were also fewer clients. In the decade and a half after World War II, when Robert Ratcliff was designing houses by the dozen, the low cost of labor and materials had made it possible to design and build an architect-designed house at reasonable cost. But with inflation in the 1960s and 1970s came a hard truth: "custom" houses were no longer competitive with the

Rotary Art and Garden Center, Live Oak Park, Berkeley, 1967. This essay in nature romanticism reprised the "tree trunk" motif of Fire Station No. 4.

mass-produced houses being built in the region's suburbs.

If the Berkeley tradition of building custom hillside houses effectively ended in the 1960s, replaced by a reverential ethos of preservation, this is not to say that the city was no longer capable of celebrating its druidic humanism in the realm of architecture. The Rotary Art and Garden Center (1967), perched above a tree-shaded creek in Live Oak Park—a hallowed site in a hillside neighborhood studded with Maybecks—enshrined the Arts and Crafts sensibilities of the Bay Tradition. The idea of creating a sylvan public setting for exhibiting and performing art was suggested at a Rotary Club meeting by Allan Temko, the noted architecture critic of the *San Francisco Chronicle* and a Berkeley resident himself. The meeting was held in Ratcliff & Ratcliff's 1957 Live Oak Park Center. With his habitual aplomb, Temko turned to Robert Ratcliff and said, "Why don't you design it?" "Sure," Ratcliff responded, not missing a beat.[17] The building, a diminutive wood pavilion with peaked roof, enclosed an open-truss hall. Structural poles ran around the building like tree trunks and provided support for the bridge—an approach that led the visitor over the creek to a deck and pergola entrance.

A similar aesthetic informed the 1965 Lake Anza bathhouses in Tilden Park. Owned and operated by the East Bay Regional Park District, the park is a wooded, two-thousand-acre expanse in the hills behind Berkeley that functions as the city's backyard, with Lake Anza as its swimming hole. Cadwalader designed the group as a diagonal row of hexagonal wood pavilions, linked at the corners; one entered through a breezeway to a patio adjoining a grassy slope leading down to the beach.

The firm's major contribution to the downtown was the Bank of California (1965), an elegantly detailed brick block pierced by tall openings with bronzed grilles, the design of Jules Kliot.[18] Murray Slama's and Peter Scott's branch office for the California State Automobile Association, from the same year, provided an oasis of architectural coherence on a ragged stretch of University Avenue a block west of the downtown.[19]

Seminary commissions built on previous work by the firm. The 1964 addition of a four-story academic building and multipurpose wing to the Berkeley Baptist Divinity School (American Baptist Seminary of the West), by Jules Kliot, comprised one the office's most sensitive contextual designs of the period. Though modern in spirit, with sleek massing and delicate corner windows, the buildings were sheathed in textured red brick to harmonize with the Tudor ensemble by Ratcliff, Haymond & Ratcliff; the design included a Gothic arcade connecting the addition to Walter Ratcliff's 1949 chapel.

During the 1960s, the firm completed several projects on the university campus. Interior alterations, including new laboratories, were made to three historic structures at the west end of the campus, formerly known as the Agriculture Group: Wellman and Hilgard Halls, designed by John Galen Howard, and Giannini Hall, by William C. Hays.[20] In 1969, construction was also completed on a press-box addition to Memorial Stadium— a dramatically cantilevered, metal-clad structure perched on the stadium's rim like a cameo of the head-on collision between the future and the past.

For the most part, however, campus-related work focused on cooperative housing projects, a communal approach to student living that resonated with the tenor of the times. Fraternity and sorority jobs dried up in the mid-1960s as those organizations entered a period of plummeting membership and heightened calumny. In one of the firm's last fraternities, Murray Slama's Phi Mu complex on Prospect Street, cockeyed steel posts were arrayed across the three-story fronts, hinting at vertiginous times to come.

With the Ridge Project, built on Holy Hill in 1966, Ratcliff, Slama & Cadwalader joined in the Brutalist chorus of the sixties campus. It was the firm's largest student housing project since Fernwald, though the client in this case was not the University of California but the University Students' Cooperative Association (USCA). This Depression-era collective, founded in Berkeley in 1934, acquired residences and apartment houses—Cloyne Court was one such acquisition— to provide affordable student lodging. Robert and his father were longtime friends with USCA's recently retired manager, Harold Norton. The Ridge Project, USCA's first attempt at new construction, contained the organization's offices, kitchen, and warehouse in addition to rooms for more than 125 students.

Its bold massing limned by rough stucco, the building peered across Hearst Avenue to the campus towers it emulated rather than the buildings it adjoined. Its closest neighbor on Ridge Road, grafted to its flank, was a half-timbered

*The three partners: Robert W. Ratcliff, Murray A. Slama,
and A. Burns Cadwalader, in the office on Adeline Street, 1970s.*

house by John Galen Howard, a survivor of the
fire; across the street was Walter Ratcliff's Church
Divinity School of the Pacific. Oblivious of the
past, but lofty in its architectural aspirations, the
Ridge Project functioned as an outpost of the
modernist campus on Holy Hill.[21]

Berkeley in the sixties became a center of
protest against the very modernism it had nurtured. Disaffected academics, beset by specters of
war, racism, and poverty, questioned the validity of
the entire modernist enterprise; cadres of scholars
condemned the rationalist paradigm as a Eurocen-
tric mindset gone awry. Student unrest added a
massed voice to the debate. Berkeley's 1964 Free
Speech Movement inaugurated the large-scale
campus sit-ins that characterized the decade, and
Mario Savio voiced what many now felt about the
technocracy: "There is a time when the operation
of the machine becomes so odious, makes you so
sick at heart, that you can't take part . . . and you've
got to put your bodies upon the gears and upon
the wheels, upon the levers, upon all the apparatus,
and you've got to make it stop."

Ratcliff, Slama & Cadwalader could not help
but be sucked into the vortex that was Berkeley in
the sixties. Soon after the completion of the Ridge
Project, the university commissioned the firm to
produce preliminary drawings for housing on a
cleared site two blocks south of campus. The
schematic designs of clustered low-rise units
on landscaped grounds demonstrated sensitivity
to site and setting, but in the polarized political
climate, design had become irrelevant. For several
months in 1969, the site, dubbed People's Park
by the protesters who set up camp there, became
a battleground where the National Guard and
Berkeley police were pitted against a heterogeneous group composed of students, activists, and
drifters. The standoff ended with a mass march
through the city that turned violent. The police
shot and killed one marcher and blinded another.
A bullet pierced the plate glass in the front window of the Ratcliff office.[22]

The office completed a final project for the
University Students' Cooperative Association.
Built in phases in 1971 and 1981, Rochdale Village
covered most of a Southside block near Telegraph
Avenue. Facing inward to landscaped courts and
screened from the street by trees, the shingled
complex of multistory buildings reprised the
Bay Tradition in a composition of cantilevered
bays and recessed balconies. In this project, care
was taken to involve the students in the design
process.[23]

RATCLIFF, Slama & Cadwalader did not achieve
this level of activity in the 1960s and 1970s without a price. For Walter Ratcliff, it had entailed a

Father and son: Walter and Robert Ratcliff in the 1960s.

painful transition at the end of his long career. Yet he was cognizant of the profound shifts that professional practice was undergoing, and he was enough of a realist to accept them gracefully. Following his retirement from the firm and the sale of the bank, he had withdrawn into a life of busy domesticity with Muriel. The children and grandchildren were frequent visitors at Roble Road, and Mendocino brought them all together for the long summers on the north coast.

Walter and Muriel's secluded cabin, with its swimming pool, ocean view, and meadow encircled by redwoods, provided a genteel contrast to Robert and Evelyn's angular shelter, bravely exposed on a scrubby, south-facing slope at the edge of a burned and logged-over forest. In completed form—it was started in the late 1940s but did not assume final shape until the 1960s— the building functioned as a gathering place for their family, its central kitchen and dining area adjoined by fireplace, lounge, deck, and bunkroom. Robert and Evelyn built another house for their

own use—the aptly named "Moon Viewing Cabin," a bold tepee of a structure with a skylight oriented to the summer moonrise—thereby freeing up the main building for the rest of the family, which had grown.

Robert and Evelyn had three more children after the war, for a total of six: Lucy, Polly, Kit, Alice, Bess, and Tom. By the early 1970s, the three older children had all married, and there were now seven grandchildren whose comings and goings enlivened the hillside house on Panoramic Way and the cabins in Mendocino. There were nieces, nephews, uncles, aunts, and cousins. The family flourished, sending out new branches.

On May 4, 1973, at the advanced age of 92, the patriarch of this clan, Walter Harris Ratcliff, died at his home on Roble Road: the house he had designed for his family, where he and Muriel had raised their five children, and where they had lived for six decades. The *Berkeley Gazette,* in a long obituary, called him someone "whose presence here vastly altered the shape of the city."[24] Less than a year later, on March 16, 1974, a month before her 82nd birthday, Muriel Cora Williams Ratcliff passed away. Her granddaughter Polly, Robert and Evelyn's second-born, had just given birth to her third child, a baby girl; and Robert and Evelyn's third-born, Kit, himself the father of two little girls, decided around this time to join the firm.

Rochdale Village, Haste Street, Berkeley, 1971. Inspired by the exploded box forms of 1960s Bay Tradition modernism, this complex (enlarged in 1981) was the firm's last dormitory project prior to Foothill Student Housing.

Six The Ratcliff Architects

UNDER Robert Ratcliff's guidance, the family firm had reinvented itself in the postwar metropolitan milieu. The proof of his success was the thriving office he brought into being: the transformation of Walter Ratcliff's waning practice into a versatile modern firm. The son carried within him an ideal that he strove to achieve in his professional and personal dealings—a fundamental seriousness about work, and life, and service that was one of his father's chief legacies.

Robert had risked everything when he took on new partners and offered them equal stakes in the firm. He didn't have to do it. He must have needed that sort of relationship, personally and professionally, to induce him to gamble with his heritage. Murray Slama and Burns Cadwalader repaid his largesse with loyalty. As the business prospered, it grew in technical and managerial complexity—more projects and more employees, three times as many in the late 1970s as in the 1960s—taxing the resources of the partnership. And there were those, including Robert's own son, who were ready to move up. The 1980s would prove to be a vital, and turbulent, chapter in the firm's history.

THROUGHOUT these years, the pace at home was equally challenging. The Ratcliff residence on Panoramic Way had been substantially enlarged after the war to accommodate the growing family. Robert and Evelyn performed a delicate pas de deux, balancing their professional and parental duties with their circle of friends, a lively group that included musicians, painters, sculptors, writers, and photographers. They hosted soirees around the grand piano in the new living room with the freestanding circular fireplace, vistas of golden lights or tangled fog beyond the windows, music, cocktails, and laughter.

The new office of The Ratcliff Architects, Doyle Street, Emeryville, 1990.

Kit (Christopher), the oldest boy, slept in a small room at the bottom of the stairs, a glassed-in porch that made him feel exposed to the world outside, inches from his face, plants and animals stirring in the night. Later he moved into another equally exposed space, the upstairs library in the new living room wing. This less than private upbringing reinforced his tendency to openness; he would remain porous to people—a believer, like his father, in the importance of community.

At the age of 17, in 1961, Kit entered UC Berkeley. He spent two years in the College of Letters and Science exploring a wide range of subjects. He then thought he would like engineering for its combination of creativity and logic, but he soon decided it was too formulaic and predictable—"I didn't want to be limited to a left-brain legacy," as he put it later—so he decided to study architecture instead. Like his father, he went into the field because somehow it felt right to him; there was no family pressure. The open-ended creativity and mystery of architecture appealed to his "right-brain" sensibilities. "I wanted to deal with the unknown," he said. He enrolled in the five-year program of the Department of Architecture in 1963, graduating with a bachelor's degree, cum laude, in 1968. Under the direction of William Wurster since 1951, the school had become a bastion of modernism, shedding the vestiges of its Beaux-Arts past. The department now formed part of an interdisciplinary program, with landscape architecture and urban planning, called the College of Environmental Design. Early in his training, in 1964, Kit moved from the Ark—the shingled complex designed by John Galen Howard where his father had studied in the 1930s—to Wurster Hall, the new home of the College of Environmental Design.

Kit loved the Ark, but it was overcrowded; some classes met in temporary wartime buildings on campus. He knew that many felt "Fort Wurster" was too aggressive in its hard-edged Brutalism, but he liked its coldness, its exacting scale and forthright use of materials, and the new sense of community it fostered among the departments of the college. Ironically, the looming concrete structure proclaimed the triumph of architectural modernism as modernism itself was in retreat.[1]

The counter-modernist paradigm that emerged forcefully in the 1960s rejected the primacy of Western thought and culture. To its adherents, the new model represented a leap in consciousness, a shift from rationalistic to holistic thinking, from exploitive to ecological practice, from a parochial to a planetary perspective. As the modernist hegemony fragmented, its single voice replaced by a competing chorus, postmodernism, so-called, was born.

The intellectual assault on modernism in the broadest sense of the term contributed to the wane of architectural modernism as a formal aesthetic, coincident with the passing of the great modernist pioneers: Wright, Gropius, Mies, and Corbusier. At leading schools, professors and students began to delve more deeply into the social dimensions of architecture. Building on the legacy of William Wurster, most architects who taught at Berkeley in the 1960s were humanists who placed a primacy on function over form; their ideal was the creation of environments for living rather than objects for viewing. Charles Moore, Joseph Esherick, Christopher Alexander, and others commingled theory and practice to arrive at an architecture that addressed the needs and aspirations of its users.

Moore and his older colleague Esherick, a disciple of the recently deceased Maybeck, were also key figures in the evolving Bay Tradition. Both architects cultivated a deferential attitude toward the natural qualities of site, and both were deeply receptive to vernacular traditions. As such, they were modern-day transmitters of the Arts and Crafts ideal—an ethos and aesthetic refined by the Bay Tradition and enshrined at Berkeley as in few other places in the world.

Among the theorists of the College of Environmental Design, it was the youngest, Alexander, who persisted most diligently, if not obsessively, in asking what it is people want in the buildings they live, work, study, heal, and worship in. He critiqued the modernist tradition as a reductionist project of the Western mind, the imposition of "top-down" concepts of space and structure to determine form. He proposed instead a "bottom-up" approach, one that would look at design problems from a multitude of angles, assembling the finished form of a building from many small pieces. His system of "pattern language" parsed the grammar of design into its fundamental parts as a basis for meaningful dialogue between client and designer. This reorientation of the role of the architect attempted to deconstruct and democratize the design process, transforming it into an inclusive act.[2]

In his writings and his own buildings, Alexander spoke a language rooted in the vernacular, in natural materials and handcrafted workmanship: an unambiguous expression of his Arts and Crafts lineage. If Esherick invigorated the Bay Tradition with Maybeckian passion, and Moore disseminated it through the cool Wursterian elegance of Sea Ranch, Alexander was its avatar, channeling and translating Berkeley's genius loci into a language that would assure the persistence of the Arts and Crafts enterprise into the twenty-first century.

As a student at Berkeley in the 1960s, Kit Ratcliff felt the full force of the emergent postmodern paradigm, just as his father had succumbed to the thrall of ascendant modernism in the 1930s, and his grandfather to the allure of academic eclecticism at the turn of the twentieth century. He resonated with Alexander's right-brain proclivities, though he chafed under his theoretical certainties. One day in class he asked, "Why not use both approaches—top-down *and* bottom-up? Why either-or when it can be both-and?" Kit also worked closely with Henry Sanoff, an instructor who saw in him an ability to make connections and "think outside of the box."

Kit married while he was in school, and by the time he graduated, he and Kate had a daughter. That summer of 1968 they left for a year in England, where he worked for a London firm whose projects included a commercial center in Cambridge. Back home, a second daughter due, he found work with Building Systems Development, a company that fostered new building technologies in federal agencies and universities. When he joined Ratcliff, Slama & Cadwalader in 1974, his timing was analogous to his father's a generation earlier: each was the beneficiary of a bequest in need of renewal, and each bore within himself seeds of change.

IN 1978, when Robert was 65, Ratcliff, Slama & Cadwalader expanded the partnership to include three new principals—Peter Scott, Don Kasamoto, and Sy Husain. To avoid the unwieldiness of five names on the letterhead, and to reinforce the firm's historic identity, the name was changed to The Ratcliff Architects.

The following year, the Berkeley Chamber of Commerce awarded Robert Ratcliff the Benjamin Ide Wheeler Public Service Award as the city's "most distinguished citizen."[3] Though he was now at the height of his renown, with a large and growing practice, he found the transition difficult: the old partnership had been his creation, and it was hard to let go. He was particularly shaken by the departure of Murray Slama—his indispensable associate of twenty-five years—who left to start his own practice soon after the new partnership was formed. A downturn in the economy added to the stress.

Then came the discovery, in 1980, that the firm's business manager was an embezzler. "I was on a holiday in Inverness when I received a phone call from Bob," Burns Cadwalader recalled. "He told me to sit down; then he told me what happened." Robert was deeply hurt by the theft—it wasn't the money so much as the sense of betrayal: that a trusted member of his "family" could do such a thing. After a period of austerity, and with the support of the firm's consultants, the company was able to pull through. "A major factor in our survival was the long-term relationships we had with the design community," said Peter Scott, who became the firm's president in 1980, as the scandal was breaking. "Because of our longevity and reliability, they stood with us through a very rough time."

The younger partners saw the embezzlement as a wake-up call that the firm needed a more structured, accountable work environment. "We became more business oriented," said Don Kasamoto. "The practice went through other changes at this time as we, and the profession as a whole, became more conscious of ever-increasing litigation against architects. We began to build our risk-management systems."

During his tenure as president, Scott took the opportunity to introduce changes he had long advocated. He saw to the hiring of administrative specialists—notably, the office's first fulltime marketing director—and oversaw the production of brochures and mailers, including an award-winning newsletter that paired images of Ratcliff buildings with essays on architectural themes.[4] In general, he promoted design and the role of designers within the firm, believing that "in the office's comforting, family-like environment, their skills did not get the attention and support they deserved." Though he never met his goal of designating a lead designer for each project—in this he was resisted by Robert, who held to his credo that "everyone is a designer"—Scott did his best to further the work of talented designers like Crodd Chin, Chuck Trevisan, David Maglaty, and Richard Bartlett. He also established an interiors department, initially under Jean Hansen, to help refine decisions relating to lighting, color, texture, fabrics, and furnishings.

As the office went through its changes under the new partners, Robert participated less and less in its affairs. Already 70 years old and approaching his fortieth year with the firm, he found himself tiring of the routine—the recurring problems, the endless round of expectations, the unending effort to create new and complex things. His retirement in 1984 recalled his father's withdrawal some thirty years before. Even so, he was unable to let go completely, and would continue going to the office. And he was still very much himself, his love of life and art intact. Peter Scott recalled with amazement how Robert spontaneously broke into song one day, harmonizing an Italian aria with a secretary who studied opera.

Scott would leave next, in 1987, during his twenty-fifth year with the firm, and in his seventh as president, to start his own practice in Berkeley. Kit Ratcliff, recently made a shareholding partner, became the CEO of The Ratcliff Architects. He was 43, and like his father at precisely that age, ready for his turn at the helm.

KIT HAD joined the firm with no agenda for the future; he simply wanted "a few years" with his father before he retired. He immersed himself in the practice, working on a wide range of projects: with Murray Slama on historical buildings at Fort Vancouver, Washington; with Sy Husain on hospitals in Salinas and Modesto; with Peter Scott on water treatment plants in the East Bay; with Burns Cadwalader on Rochdale Village II in Berkeley.

So it was that Kit Ratcliff became part of the

Robert and Kit Ratcliff, early 1980s.

The firm's six principals in the late 1970s— Syed V. Husain, Peter Gray Scott, and Donald T. Kasamoto (seated); Robert W. Ratcliff, A. Burns Cadwalader, and Murray A. Slama (standing).

firm. The life of the company would increasingly intertwine itself with his own: the embezzlement coincided with a divorce; his rise to leadership accompanied his remarriage. His wife, Janet Tam, was a graduate of the College of Environmental Design, with a master's degree in architecture. She would go on to establish her own Berkeley firm, Noll & Tam, in the early 1990s, following the birth of their two daughters.

The Ratcliff Architects took on larger and more complex projects in the 1980s, and the office approached one hundred employees by the end of the decade. By the standards of the industry, the practice was still "midsized": larger than the legion of start-ups that populated the region, yet nowhere near the size of corporate firms like HOK or SOM. Ratcliff derived its uniqueness from its culture, its ethos of community, as well as from its longevity and multigenerational heritage, which commanded respect and imbued its work, however contemporary, with the texture of time. The new terminal at Oakland International Airport, opened in 1985, was the signature work of the decade, as important to the firm as Highland Hospital had been in the 1960s or the Chamber of Commerce Building in the 1920s. The terminal project "put us on the map in our profession and was the start of a number of larger projects that characterized the 1980s," Kit Ratcliff recalled.

Like hospitals and university campuses, airports were symbols of modern technocratic culture: air travel proliferated in tandem with the civilization it served. The advent of jet transports in the 1950s democratized flight—larger and faster planes meant more passengers on more frequent trips, reducing the price of tickets. By the mid-1980s, the Bay Area's three major airports (San Francisco, Oakland, and San Jose) served thirty million passengers annually, three times as many as in 1960s.[5]

In the 1970s, the Port of Oakland, which administers the airport, began planning for a new terminal to serve the jaunty "commuter" carriers that were its top revenue producers, Pacific Southwest Airlines and Air California. The Ratcliff office, which had never designed anything remotely resembling an airport, approached the job as a do-or-die effort. The initial contact came through Cadwalader, who knew several port officials. Kasamoto, the principal in charge, served as project manager, and it was his cost analysis that convinced the port to double its budget. Kit Ratcliff oversaw the completion of the project. The initial scheme was rejected, leading to Crodd Chin's breakthrough design. A member of the firm since 1970, four years after his graduation with a bachelor's degree in architecture from UC Berkeley, Chin had honed his skills on a variety of projects. He came into his own on the terminal project.

The building combined structural and spatial drama. The high, open trusses of the space frame spanned the "great hall" of the check-in and baggage-claim areas, which led to the nearby mezzanine gates. Space compressed as one moved from the "hall" to the waiting areas, and finally into the aircraft itself.

Allan Temko's influential "Environmental Design" column in the *San Francisco Chronicle* praised

Mezzanine restaurant and shops above baggage claim area,
Terminal 2, Oakland International Airport, 1985.

Terminal 2, Oakland International Airport

Arrowhead Marsh Visitor Center, Martin Luther King, Jr.,
Regional Shoreline, Oakland, 1983.

the building as "just about the finest facility of its kind in the country." Temko described "a single luminous space" with "the same subdued palette of silvery grays, handsome stucco and metal set off by fine hardware of stainless steel." He referred to the space-frame structure as "an extremely efficient, lightweight system of interacting trusses. They are not governed by any directional pattern, but can advance as a spatial continuum, framed by diagonal members, spanning large spaces at low cost." The final cost of the terminal, about $17 million, was indeed low for a structure enclosing 100,000 square feet. At the end of the piece, Temko voiced a Berkeleyan's appreciation of the Ratcliff heritage: "It's heartening to think of the continuity of this family firm over three generations. Founded early in the century by Walter Ratcliff, designer of some of Berkeley's best buildings, the firm maintained its tradition under his son, Robert Ratcliff. And the airport project has been headed by his son, Kit Ratcliff."[6]

Terminal 2 at Oakland Airport represented the firm at its most heroically modern. Under the waning influence of Robert Ratcliff and Burns Cadwalader, the woodsy romanticism of the Bay Tradition had lingered on in the firm's work, but faintly, as if marginalized by the realities of metropolitan growth. Several young designers kept the tradition alive in the 1980s. David Maglaty's Elmwood Village (1983)—one of the firm's finest small projects of the period—occupied a narrow infill lot next to Berkeley's Elmwood Theater, fitting quietly into the historic commercial district. Entered through an archway, the two-level complex of wood-clad shops and offices faced inward to a meandering lane with walkways crossing overhead. Gables, windows, and other elements were shrunk, making the restricted site seem larger, a manipulation of space and scale recalling both Coxhead and Maybeck.[7] The Arrowhead Marsh Visitor Center, erected in 1983 for the East Bay Regional Park District, months before Robert Ratcliff's retirement, embodied the Arts and Crafts ethos. Largely the design of Richard Bartlett, the sloping, rough, all-wood structure had an elegiac quality that paid homage to its setting, an island of nature in an urban sea.[8]

RATCLIFF's expertise in health care, inaugurated in the 1960s by the Highland Hospital addition, continued to expand under Husain's guidance. By the early 1980s, projects had been completed in many cities in northern California, including Salinas, Stockton, and Modesto. The most important client of the decade was the Veterans Administration (VA), the federal government's principal health care provider.[9] The VA Palo Alto Surgical Addition, a $16-million project that ranked as one of the firm's largest (comparable to the Oakland Airport terminal) had lasting consequences in terms of further work with the VA and new commissions from Kaiser Permanente and other providers.

Acute Care Facility, California Veterans Home, Yountville, 1988. Old and new blend harmoniously in this Napa Valley complex.

Parking structure for Children's Hospital, Oakland, 1991. The last of several projects begun in the 1980s for this hospital, with Kava Massih as lead designer, the structure has varied façades that respond to the setting. According to Massih, the west elevation was rendered in "a few bold strokes" to allow it to be read quickly by passing BART trains.

In the mid-1980s, following the completion of the surgical addition, the VA contracted with Ratcliff (in association with Stone, Marraccini & Patterson) to begin planning for other alterations and additions to the Palo Alto campus, the largest VA facility in northern California. Following the 1989 Loma Prieta earthquake, the firm enabled continuous operations at the damaged hospital through the rapid installation of modular buildings. At the same time, the VA commissioned Ratcliff to design replacements for significant elements of the campus, including a diagnostic radiation center, clinical/bed wing, and administration building. Completed in phases in the 1990s, the $140-million project was far and away the largest in the firm's history.

A smaller VA project, completed in 1988 at a cost of $8.8 million, was a case study in nuanced design by David Maglaty. This acute-care addition formed part of the California Veterans Home, a retirement facility in Yountville, at the center of the Napa Valley. Dating from the 1930s, the Spanish-style complex sat on a knoll surrounded by vineyards. The stucco-and-tile imagery of the new wing, conspicuously sited at the front of the campus, blended with the old buildings, while its crisply gabled forms conveyed a contemporary spirit. Care was taken with the interior design to avoid a high-tech, institutional look. Colors and finishes were chosen to create a comfortable ambience for the elderly resident population and the patient-friendly plan included a logical progression of uses. Natural light filled the atrium lobby, streaming through windows oriented to vistas of the wine country.[10]

THE RATCLIFF Architects worked on a succession of academic facilities in the 1980s, culminating in major projects that set the stage for its expanded academic practice in the following decade. The firm continued to move beyond its established base of operations, at UC Berkeley and the University of the Pacific, to other campuses of the UC system, and for the first time completed a major project outside of California.

The first academic project to come out of the office in the 1980s was the Science Engineering Center at Humboldt State University, in the coastal city of Arcata, near Eureka. The firm had won the contract in a design competition in the late 1970s, with Peter Scott as head of the competition team and Richard Bartlett as chief designer. A high-tech, linear composition of distinct parts—geodesic dome, gabled sheds, and a curving, glass-walled section incorporating passive solar features—the building was intended as a "hands-on environmental research tool." Its occupants could regulate the ambient temperature, for example, by interacting with the zero-mass Trombe glazed walls—a milestone in the firm's evolving commitment to sustainable, green design.

Contextual concerns were uppermost in the design of a new music center for the University of the Pacific. Opened in 1986, the ensemble of gabled, red-brick buildings faced the historic campus green, complementing the university's traditional Tudor styling. Designed by Bill Blessing, a young architect who had recently joined the firm, the project recalled in contemporary fashion Ratcliff, Haymond & Ratcliff's sensitive additions

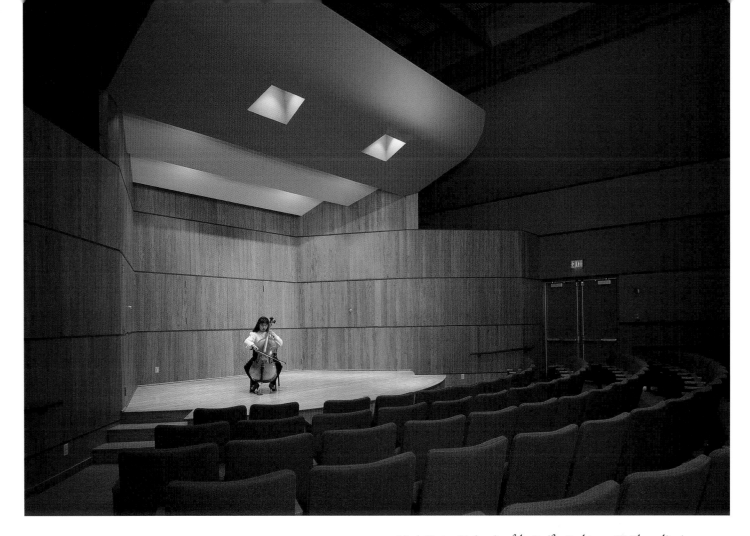

Music Center, University of the Pacific, Stockton, 1986. The auditorium was the firm's first performance hall since the Mills College Music Building.

to the Baptist School of Divinity some thirty years earlier.

As the Oakland terminal neared completion late in 1984, the firm won its most important academic commission of the decade: a $33-million science complex at the University of Oregon comprising four new buildings along with additions and alterations. The project involved master planning, site studies, programming, and a design process that utilized pattern language to articulate the concerns of faculty, students,

administrators, and community representatives.[11] Ratcliff collaborated with Charles Moore (Moore Ruble Yudell) and Brockmeyer McDonnell, serving as executive architect with responsibility for project management. The eclectic postmodern ensemble, grouped around a spectacular atrium and stairway, was rendered in warm red brick that harmonized with the older buildings of the Eugene campus.

Science Engineering Center, Humboldt State University, Arcata, 1981.
This was the firm's first major project to incorporate sustainable design principles.

Science Complex, University of Oregon, 1990. A collaborative undertaking with Moore Ruble Yudell and Brockmeyer McDonnell, this was the firm's principal academic project of the 1980s.

The Ratcliff Architects entered into other collaborations on major academic projects in the late 1980s, including the Molecular Biology Research Laboratory II at UC San Diego and the Psychiatric Inpatient Facility at UC Irvine (both with Moore Ruble Yudell), and Foothill Student Housing at UC Berkeley (with William Turnbull Associates).[12] Though Foothill was beset by bureaucratic and legal muddle, the $30-million job was the Berkeley campus's biggest housing project of the 1980s, and it reinforced the firm's historic ties to the university.

RATCLIFF also established itself as a player in the burgeoning field of historic preservation, a counter-modernist movement that gained momentum in the 1970s. As old buildings were seen with new eyes, valued for their architectural qualities and historical associations, a new sector of the profession began specializing in the documentation and rehabilitation of historic structures.

With its rich legacy of historic architecture, the Bay Area was a national center of the movement. Citizen groups like the Berkeley Architectural Heritage Association (BAHA) conducted neighborhood surveys, held annual home tours, and lobbied to preserve threatened landmarks.[13] A growing number of public and private property owners, in some cases subsidized by federal grants and tax incentives, opted for rehabilitation and reuse over demolition and new construction. By the time Ratcliff began taking on such projects in the 1970s, several small Bay Area firms had carved

Foothill Student Housing, University of California, Berkeley, 1990. Designed in collaboration with William Turnbull Associates, this remains the largest of the firm's dormitory projects.

The 1981 rehabilitation of the Hotel Oakland, a 1912 landmark by the firm of Bliss & Faville, resulted in 315 units of senior housing.

out a niche in the field, but few general practitioners had the inclination or the skills to follow suit. Slama, however, with his omnivorous professionalism, opened the door by becoming conversant in preservation work.[14]

Ratcliff's major rehabilitation projects of the 1980s were in Oakland. The earliest, completed in 1981, was the HUD-financed conversion of the Hotel Oakland to senior housing. Erected in 1912, the monumental structure was one of the city's principal downtown landmarks. Ratcliff reinforced the steel-frame, brick-clad structure for earthquake safety, renovated the ornate lobby and ballroom, and converted the upper floors to 315 apartments.[15] A similar project, from 1987, involved the rehabilitation of the California Hotel, an abandoned 1929 building also renovated for low-income housing. The firm's most daunting preservation project of the decade was the H. J. Kaiser Convention Center, commissioned by Oakland's city government. Facing Lake Merritt near the Alameda County courthouse, the massive Beaux-Arts structure, built prior to World War I as the Oakland Civic Auditorium, had suffered from years of neglect and misguided improvements. The rehabilitation included a seismic retrofit, restoration of character-defining features, and renovation for adaptive reuse as a convention facility. The project received two AIA awards for excellence in design.

IN 1990, after nearly thirty years in one location, the firm moved one mile west to its current offices in a renovated warehouse in Emeryville. Wedged between Berkeley and Oakland, this small city had once been an industrial enclave of canneries and factories. It was now something else: an assemblage of stylish condominiums, offices, and malls in new and converted buildings, emblematic of recent development trends in the region's historic cities. The office itself achieved a balance between new and old, sharp-edged partitions within exposed brick walls.

It was no accident that the move happened when it did. Like Robert Ratcliff's change of location after assuming control of Ratcliff & Ratcliff, this was Kit Ratcliff's way of laying claim to The Ratcliff Architects as the firm approached its second century.

THE RATCLIFF Architects entered the 1990s with bright prospects. Ensconced in its spacious new offices in Emeryville, its staff larger than ever, the firm prospered through its burgeoning health care and academic practices; never before had so many important projects been started or recently completed. The contrast with the uncertain state of the business a decade earlier, at the outset of the eighties, was nothing less than remarkable. A strong economy enabled the turnaround, but the company could not have grown without the focused effort of its principals, not least its CEO, Kit Ratcliff.

The new decade would usher in its own set of challenges, confronting the partners once again with the exigencies of change. In the wake of a weakened economy, the company would downsize and merge with a San Francisco firm. By 2000, it would reemerge with a new leadership team, a workforce of about seventy-five, and a new name—Ratcliff—prepared to do business in the twenty-first century.

IN THE architectural profession, sons have sometimes succeeded fathers—Eero Saarinen and John Carl Warnecke famously come to mind—but a third generation in the same office is exceedingly rare. Leadership of successful architectural firms requires vision and charisma, in addition to professional aptitude and acumen: a blend of latent and learned qualities developed over a lifetime, not received as a birthright. A sense of entitlement may provide the confidence to assume a leading role, but it does not guarantee that the part will be played well.

When Robert succeeded Walter Ratcliff, he succeeded forcefully, transforming a shrunken firm into a midsized office. His name and leadership

skills, together with the stability of the partnership and manageable scale of operations, were the ingredients of this success. But the cozy, chummy management style he fostered at Ratcliff & Ratcliff, and later at Ratcliff, Slama & Cadwalader, became less effective as the business grew; by the late 1970s, with the advent of The Ratcliff Architects, it was a liability—a state of affairs underscored by the embezzlement.

When Kit Ratcliff became the firm's president, having witnessed the transition to a five-person, then a six-person, and finally a four-person partnership, the company was larger than ever, its work far more complex. The design process, from master planning and programming to implementation, had become a more regulated team effort, with delineated roles and hierarchies, particularly for large institutional projects: a world away from the free-spirited, "everyone is a designer" ethos of earlier years. Then, projects were divvied up among the principals, who assembled their teams informally; there was a fluid exchange of members from team to team. Now each team had an array of managers and tasks. The principal in charge, who usually made the initial contact with the client, attended key meetings and generally tracked progress. Most responsibility fell on the shoulders of the project manager, who estimated costs, generated submittal schedules, administered contracts, dealt with consultants, and in general provided hands-on oversight. The project architect assembled the design team, made sure drawings and other project documents were delivered on schedule, monitored the quality of the work, and served as the day-to-day point person. The

team itself, which could number as many as twenty people, consisted of a project designer along with technical and design support staff. These changes in the practice reflected the increased complexity and formality of the profession at large, embedded as it was in a bureaucratized, technical culture.

A proliferation of tasks—promoting the business, putting out proposals, writing contracts, responding to regulatory issues, getting permits, attending to client needs, supervising construction, running computer systems, managing money, managing risk—created a bevy of positions. It was no longer possible for one person to master the field, as had been the case in Walter's day, or even in the early years of Robert's career; in order to survive, let alone thrive, the firm had to assemble a management team of complementary experts to oversee a workforce of diverse specialists.

For Kit Ratcliff, the generalist in this picture, it was less a matter of reinventing a business stuck in the past, as his father had done, than it was taking the helm of a functioning company that needed to be steered toward the future. He embraced new technologies and new concepts. Yet his leadership style was discreet, tending toward consensus. He ascribed to the so-called Toyota model of manufacturing: if you find an error in the system, you can shut it down to learn why it failed. His holistic vision, informed by voracious reading and wide-ranging conversation, saw the company as a living entity, an organism with the potential to reach new levels of productivity.[1] To this end, he became

The glass-enclosed circulation mall of the Kaiser Medical Center, Fresno.

equal parts matchmaker and alchemist, always seeking the next new person, adjusting and calibrating the mix to elicit a golden glow of synergy. Annual retreats to the family ranch in Mendocino, a tradition since the 1970s, made the process all the more enjoyable.

"I am a person first and an architect second," he is prone to say. "I want to know why people think and act the way they do. I want to understand why the company works, and why it doesn't. I want to understand my clients, and I want them to know me. Together we can learn to ask the right questions, identify the right problems, and arrive at the right solutions."

Thus far his career had unfolded without undue setback: his twenties spent as a student and fledgling architect, his thirties getting established in the practice, his forties a harvest of professional achievement—a chronology closely paralleling his father's. This would all change during his third decade at the firm, when he found himself scrambling for work and looking for partners in a drifting economy. As had happened repeatedly in the firm's roller-coaster history—no different from the profession at large—it came down to a question of survival.

By the early 1990s, three of The Ratcliff Architects' four partners were on their way out. The oldest, Burns Cadwalader, retired in 1992 at the age of 77, after thirty-one years as a principal; the two other senior partners, Sy Husain and Don Kasamoto, were in their sixties and contemplating retirement. None of this was unforeseen. Soon after becoming CEO, Kit Ratcliff had initiated

what was to become a lengthy discussion among the partners concerning the need for renewed leadership. Finally, in 1993, seven members of the firm were invited to become principals, upping the total to ten.[2]

By the time the selection process had run its course, the economy had taken a downturn; work tapered off to such a degree that the number of employees dropped to below fifty, less than half the peak level of the 1980s. "It was a very unstable time for the firm," Kit Ratcliff remembered:

We had far too many new principals come on board at once, given the declining number of old principals. They didn't particularly get along with one another, and there wasn't enough core left to really hold them together. As the firm began to wind down from the great jobs it had all through the 1980s and into the 1990s, we became top-heavy with partners who weren't able to get enough work to keep them all busy. It all began to unravel.[3]

The new principals declined offers to become shareholders and most left; only Crodd Chin remained. "From mid-1993 to late 1995 was a very difficult time personally, getting work and sleeping," Ratcliff recalled. It was around this time that the firm began considering a merger: a radical intervention that promised renewal but also risked further disruption. The partners surveyed a number of firms and made several overtures, but the breakthrough came unbidden, during a competition for a new state office building in San Francisco.

The Ratcliff Architects did not get that job, but it brought Kit Ratcliff into contact with Pam Helmich, whose San Francisco firm, Crosby

Helmich Architects, was on the same team. On the advice of Rich Pipkin, a managerial consultant to architectural and engineering firms, Ratcliff initiated talks with Helmich and her partner, Don Crosby: "We seemed to get along quite well and after several meetings decided to introduce the shareholders of each firm to one another." The Ratcliff Architects and Crosby Helmich pursued the talks into the waning months of 1995, arriving at an agreement late in the year. The actual merger, which occurred in February 1996, brought around twenty-five people to the firm, bringing the workforce up to about seventy-five. The company retained the name The Ratcliff Architects.

The new partners also brought in considerable expertise, as well as clients. Don Crosby had built a strong reputation over the course of a thirty-five-year career. A native of Los Angeles who attended Stanford on a football scholarship, earning his degree in architecture in 1960, he became a founding partner in the San Francisco firm of Crosby Thornton Hill Associates in 1965, when he was 28. The office prospered designing big residential subdivisions and later branched into public work, ski resorts, and professional sports facilities.

The merger did not occur without adjustments. Several factors turned the transition into a protracted affair that took several years to sort out. Chief among these was the economy. "As we ran low on work and fell on hard times, relationships started to deteriorate," Ratcliff said. "By May 1997, Pam had decided to resign from her role as chief operating officer." Disappointed by the failure of the collaboration, Ratcliff nevertheless felt that her brief tenure bore fruit: "In retrospect, she brought a new sense of a single firm rather than the duchies of former years."

Helmich's departure was followed in quick succession by the retirements of Sy Husain, in 1998 at age 70, and Don Kasamoto, in 1999 at 65, after twenty-year tenures as principals. The profound sense of passage was compounded by the deaths of Robert and Evelyn Ratcliff. Evelyn was 83 when she died in 1997, on Panoramic Way, her grandchildren gathered at her bedside. Six months later, Robert died in a Berkeley hospital, a week before his 85th birthday.

THROUGH all this, Kit Ratcliff persisted in rebuilding the firm, bringing in new principals as owners. By 2000, the transition had stabilized at seven shareholding partners. Ratcliff remained president and CEO. Crosby oversaw project and risk management. Crodd Chin remained the firm's senior designer. David Dersch was the chief financial officer, Carolyn Silk chief operating officer, and Gary Burk manager of health care planning.[4]

David Dersch, who in 1997 became the firm's first non-architect partner, was a financial manager who had begun his career as a corporate accountant. He gained entree to the architectural community working at Rich Pipkin's company, A/E Resources, which had handled the Crosby Helmich merger in 1989. Dersch subsequently joined that firm as business manager, becoming a partner, principal, and chief financial officer. Carolyn Silk, a graduate of Yale who practiced in Seattle for many years, joined Ratcliff in 1996 "because of the strong alignment I felt with the values of the leaders of the firm." She was made principal and COO the following year and partner in 1998, the year Sy Husain retired.

After the merger, the most pressing issue for Kit Ratcliff was finding a replacement for Husain. A pillar of the firm for thirty years, the architect had shepherded Ratcliff's health care work from a single project to a robust share—over half—of the company's revenues.[5] Ratcliff's choice was Gary Burk, who brought to the job experience as an academic, practicing architect, and health care planner in corporate and consulting offices across the country. In addition to becoming the principal in charge of health care, he was made managing partner of a new branch of the business, Ratcliff Consulting Services, providing comprehensive planning services to medical clients.

At the outset of the new century, the partners chose a simpler name for the firm to encompass its multifaceted nature—its emphases on architectural, consulting, and interior services—conveying in a single word a sense of continuity and change, of a passing generation and a new beginning, and of a family: Ratcliff.

BY THE end of the twentieth century, the Ratcliff name was associated with health care facilities across northern California, from full-service hospitals to medical office buildings, clinics, and laboratories. That this occurred at all was due to the realities of life in a metropolitan region with millions of people facing health issues every day.

In America, where well-being is big business, health care has become an industry of overlapping bureaucracies, epitomized by the health management organization (HMO): highly technical in its regulatory and programmatic requirements, tightly bound by the risks of liability. Architects who enter this realm risk becoming captive to its complexities and constraints, turned into functionaries of institutional power (a danger in any profession). Yet it is also possible, with persistence and intelligence, to attain that high level of competence and creativity called mastery (the promise of every profession). Such an architect possesses the potential to work with any client on terms of mutual respect, and may be able to persuade powerful institutions to collaborate in the creation of buildings of durable value.

Ratcliff strove to be such a firm: a humanizing force in institutional environments. What Husain had described as his "holistic, patient-centered approach" influenced other architects in the firm, and the overall quality of health care work, from new buildings on new sites to expansions of older facilities, had steadily improved over the years. Additions became increasingly contextual, responding to their settings with continuities of massing, material, and color that sought the harmony of the whole. Interiors achieved greater clarity of plan and ease of circulation; the soothing confluence of light, color, and texture was evident in public areas and private rooms alike.

Yet in the context of the overall design process,

Trauma/Critical Care Building, Community Medical Centers, Fresno, 2005, in association with RTKL. This facility is the first phase in a master plan for a 58-acre campus that will consolidate the Fresno Community Medical Center, University Medical Center, and UC San Francisco medical education program at Fresno.

Kaiser Medical Office Building, Santa Rosa, 2003. The design team produced a lively façade for this building in a rapidly growing section of the city.

projects that resulted from this search for the right problems to solve were in the Ratcliff tradition— a client-based, functional, dignified architecture, appropriate to health care's gravitas.

Kaiser Permanente, the nation's largest not-for-profit HMO, had been a Ratcliff client since the 1970s. Founded in 1945, the Oakland-based health plan was an outgrowth of workers' programs at Henry J. Kaiser's construction, manufacturing, and shipbuilding companies during the Depression and World War II. By 2005, the system served over eight million members in nine states, employing over eleven thousand physicians in its thirty regional medical centers and over four hundred medical office buildings. Most of Kaiser Permanente's facilities remain in California, where three-fourths of its subscribers live.

Ratcliff's contracts with Kaiser proliferated after the 1980s. Nine projects were completed between 1990 and 2006 at a total construction cost of $230 million. The biggest job by far in this renewed collaboration was the new $80 million medical center in Fresno, built in phases between 1990 and 1994. The firm's stated goal—"to create an appealing, noninstitutional environment with the potential for future expansion and flexibility of change"—was realized in the streamlined styling, dispersed massing, and carefully wrought interiors of the 400,000-square-foot complex. The center included a full-service hospital, a support wing for inpatient and outpatient diagnosis and treatment, and a medical office wing that could be expanded by the addition of multistory "pods." An L-shaped, glass-lined mall linked the three sections, providing circulation for staff, patients, and visitors.

these tangible results were the tip of the proverbial iceberg, the superstructure on a foundation of meticulous preparation. By the turn of the twenty-first century, health care planning, as practiced by Burk and his peers, had evolved into a computer-driven process that utilized facility assessment, operational modeling, space programming, process mapping, and client-group surveys to produce the master plans that were the basis of the design. The

Kit Ratcliff considers Kaiser Fresno "one of the highlights of my career . . . a truly wonderful collaboration between architect, contractor, and client. My sense is that we weren't supposed to have done as well as we did; today that campus is acknowledged by Kaiser as one of their best." One of his reasons for liking the project so much is that it modeled his ideal of synergistic action at a technically demanding level: "Stephanie Bartos did a great job as project manager; Crodd assumed a campus diagram from Ariane Zand and designed truly great campus architecture; other leaders included Bill Wong and David Thruston. Though very complicated as a fast track, it was finished on time and $2 million of contingencies were given back." The project was also one of the firm's first to utilize computer-assisted design (CAD), a revolutionary tool that equips architects with a digital array of graphic elements that can be assembled much faster than lines drawn on paper. Crodd Chin, among others, embraced the new technology.

Two medical office buildings completed in 2003, in the rapidly growing North Bay cities of Petaluma and Santa Rosa, serve as excellent examples of the sort of second-tier facilities maintained by Kaiser in conjunction with its regional centers. Each cost about $12 million; each enclosed a little less than 60,000 square feet, primarily outpatient clinics; and each was intended as the first unit of a master-planned campus. Exterior treatments were carefully modulated in response to site and design review. In Petaluma, the structure was sheathed in brick to reflect the historic urban setting. The Santa Rosa facility occupied a largely open site that served as a gateway to a developing section of the city. In a design process led by Bill Blessing, the project team made use of photomontages (computer renderings dropped into digital images of the site) to create a building distinguished by crisply detailed planar geometry.

Ratcliff completed projects for other Bay Area HMOs, such as ValleyCare Health System, Sutter Health, and John Muir Health. A $20-million addition to Pleasanton's ValleyCare Medical Center more than doubled its inpatient capacity. Opened in phases in 2000 and 2003, the building was clad in brick to harmonize with existing materials, and it was connected to the old hospital by a glass-and-steel rotunda that became the new entrance to the campus, enclosing a lofty, wood-paneled lobby. Chin's use of the entry rotunda as a hub for future expansion was an effective solution to one of the chief problems facing hospitals in twenty-first century California: the phased replacement of old wings made obsolete by new seismic standards.

Ratcliff's health care practice had been launched by public contracts, and a significant portion of its work remained in the public sector. The firm's long association with Alameda County—extending back to its first health care project, the 1960s expansion of Highland Hospital—resulted in a commission to consolidate the county's mental health services into a single inpatient facility. Opened in 1992, the 71,000-square-foot John George Psychiatric Pavilion occupied one corner of the spacious campus of Fairmont Hospital. Care was taken to fashion an environment that was noninstitutional and nonthreatening. The result, an ensemble of low-rise buildings, piazzas, and arcades grouped around a central green, was both pleasing and poignant in its attempt create a self-contained world, a village-like refuge for the troubled human beings committed there. The stucco-clad, metal-roofed buildings alluded to the Spanish styling of the older sections of the campus, and color was used throughout to serene effect: sandy beige, clay red, and lichen green on exteriors, muted pastels splashed by pools of indirect light within.

By contrast, the design of the hospital replacement for the Veterans Administration Medical Center in Palo Alto, a sprawling complex affiliated with the Stanford University School of Medicine, proclaimed its institutional function. At 620,000 square feet, it was the largest project in the firm's history, and the longest: begun in the mid-1980s, "fast-tracked" after the 1989 Loma Prieta earthquake, and finally brought to completion in 1997 in collaboration with Stone, Marraccini & Patterson (now Smith Group). Three massive structures—a 228-bed inpatient clinical wing, a radiology center, and an administration building, linked by bridges on four levels—rose from the campus at the head of the main drive, serving as the new centerpiece. Brick and stucco unified the group; rounded motifs provided focus. High bowed bays wrapped around a fountain court in the clinical/bed wing, enclosing light-filled alcoves along corridors. The clarity and harmony of the interiors, from lobbies and lecture halls to laboratories

Veterans Administration Medical Center, Palo Alto, 1997. Designed in collaboration with Stone, Marraccini & Patterson, VA Palo Alto remains the single largest health care undertaking in Ratcliff's history.

Main lobby of the Veterans Administration Medical Center, Palo Alto.

Admitting & Eligibility/
Urgent Care

and patients' rooms, invested a public institution with dignity.

Recent projects, such as the implementation plan for a $600-million, 600-bed replacement proposed for the Alta Bates Summit Medical Center in Oakland, underscore the expanding scale and cost of modern health care. The expansion of another East Bay HMO, Walnut Creek's John Muir Health, scheduled for completion in 2008, will serve as a state-of-the-art model of Ratcliff's evolving, patient-centered architecture. Chin's unifying rotunda, around which new and old wings are grouped, will facilitate the hospital's phased reconstruction. The rotunda itself is planned as an open well to the sky, a kinetic core of moving water and changing light, with a shadow dance of bamboo playing across its translucent surface.

RATCLIFF's principal academic commissions of the 1980s, comprising six major projects, one at the University of Oregon and five others on four of the campuses of the University of California, were all brought to completion in the early 1990s, at a total construction cost of about $175 million.

The development of the Berkeley campus and its environs had resumed in the 1980s with a sustained energy not seen since the 1960s. New academic buildings rose in clusters, and new residential compounds went up in the neighborhoods. Though these more recent buildings tended to be more nuanced in design, they were massive in scale. Foothill Student Housing, the Ratcliff-Turnbull project completed in 1990, was a case in point. With its shingle veneer, gable roofs,

Student Center, De La Salle High School, Concord. Scheduled for completion in 2006, the building (shown here in mixed-media rendering) forms part of Phase I construction in a twenty-year master plan for the campus.

Proposed ambulatory care facility (computer rendering, 2004). "The design explores the architectural expression of the entry lobby as a key element of way-finding," according to the project designer, D. Roger Hay. "At night, the columnar feature acts as a lantern signaling the public pedestrian and automobile entries, without reliance on traditional signage."

and stepped profile, the ensemble paid homage to Berkeley's Arts and Crafts heritage; yet it enclosed a quarter-million square feet and housed eight hundred students—comparable, in size and capacity, to the high-rise dormitory complexes erected in the Southside in the 1950s and 1960s.

St. Perpetua Catholic Church, Lafayette. Along with a conceptual design for the new sanctuary (shown here in watercolor rendering), Ratcliff produced a master plan in 2002 to improve existing facilities and outdoor spaces.

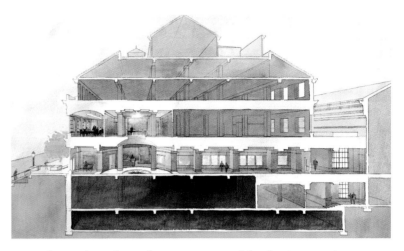

Sectional watercolor rendering of Doe Annex, UC Berkeley, showing renovations scheduled for completion in 2008. Designed in association with Noll & Tam, the improvements include renovated interior spaces, new building systems, and a new public corridor connecting with the Doe Library.

Computer rendering of open-air rotunda proposed for new wing of John Muir Health, Walnut Creek; scheduled for completion in 2008.

Watercolor rendering of Rehaboth School, village of Bugembe, Jinga, Uganda. Scheduled for completion in 2006, the school is intended primarily for orphaned children who have lost their parents to AIDS. Ratcliff was the master-plan architect, in collaboration with Ugandan architect Philip Kivunike.

The complexities of contemporary campus planning were apparent in the new facilities of the Department of Integrative Biology, a reorganized department consolidating over a dozen former departments. Costing well over $100 million, the project combined an array of new construction with the renovation of the Life Sciences Building. Opened in 1930, this brooding relic of institutional growth remained the most massive structure on campus, some 500 feet long by 250 feet wide, enclosing nearly 350,000 square feet on its five floors. Designed by George W. Kelham, Howard's successor as UC Berkeley's supervising architect, the classicist pile was overlain with stylized ornament redolent of the period's revivalist impulses, while its symmetry and axial siting adhered to Howard's Beaux-Arts plan.

In 1989, following the addition of a new laboratory wing, Ratcliff was awarded the contract to renovate the building—the largest rehabilitation ever attempted by the university.[6] Brought to completion in 1995, this project resulted in a totally new facility within the shell of the old. Sy Husain oversaw the effort as principal in charge; Linda Mahle was project manager; Chin led the design team with Dan Wetherell and Bill Blessing in support roles. The interior was gutted and rebuilt to house approximately fifty laboratories as well as auditoriums, classrooms, offices, research centers, and a library. A light court at the center of the building was partially enclosed with 60,000 square feet of infill construction that included an expanded biosciences library and a dramatic atrium with circular stairway opening onto a courtyard: a gathering place commensurate with the scale of the structure. The exterior was left unchanged except for the addition of new entrances at the centers of the long façades.[7]

A concurrent project completed in 1996 involved the renovation and expansion of the Boalt School of Law at the southeast corner of the campus. The firm was awarded the commission as part of the winning team, with Charles Pankow Builders, in a design-build competition. Under the design guidance of Crodd Chin, the 1950s building was enlarged with a 50,000-square-foot rear addition for a faculty library and offices. The adjacent Simon Hall, a 1960s dormitory tower for law students, was converted for use as offices, lounges, and childcare.[8]

The most recent campus project (slated for completion in 2008) consists of seismic and programmatic improvements to Doe Annex, home of the Bancroft Library. Built shortly after World War II as an addition to Doe Memorial Library, the five-story structure (including two subsurface floors) faced east to the Campanile's landscaped esplanade. The sensitivity of the site, adjoined by two masterworks by John Galen Howard, elicited a respectful Beaux-Arts response from Supervising Architect Arthur Brown, Jr., Kelham's successor to the post.[9] As in the case of the Valley Life Sciences Building, the project will result in a total reconstruction of the interior, leaving the exterior essentially unchanged. Leading the Ratcliff design team is Blessing, with the

Valley Life Sciences Building, University of California, Berkeley, 1995. In this night view, the new atrium space is visible through the courtyard skylight.

Berkeley firm of Noll & Tam serving in the capacity of associate architect.

Ratcliff projects on other University of California campuses included the expansion of the Pentland Hills Undergraduate Housing at UC Riverside, a 1,132-bed complex designed as a village-like ensemble in a gently sloping arroyo, completed in phases in 2000 and 2003. The firm also designed two facilities for the UC Davis campus: the Equine Performance Laboratory opened in 2005, and the new Western Human Nutrition Research Center for the U.S. Department of Agriculture was completed in 2006.

Other projects in the Bay Area allowed the firm to become more fluent in contextual neohistoricism. The Music and Dance Building at Santa Clara University, completed in 1999, employed a stucco-and-tile idiom in harmony with the prevailing style of the 1920s campus. The same approach was taken in a pair of post-2000 projects at St. Mary's College, in the East Bay suburb of Moraga, a campus of similar age and style. The new Science Center (Brother Alfred Brousseau Hall, formerly J. C. Gatehouse Hall) displayed an assured handling of compositional and ornamental elements, and the design concept for Filippi Academic Hall, housing the School of Education, incorporated Spanish Colonial motifs to enhance its presence on the campus's historic quad. Blessing led the design team on both projects.

Other academic projects employed a modernist vocabulary suited to their settings. For Oakland's Laney College, in the Peralta Community College

Atrium stairway of the renovated Valley Life Sciences Building.

Science Center (Brother Alfred Brousseau Hall), St. Mary's College, Moraga, 2001. The neo-Spanish styling evokes an earlier chapter in the firm's history.

District, the firm transformed a former welding shop into a stylish computer technology center, completed in 2001. Peralta was also the client for the new campus of Berkeley City College (formerly Vista College). This project, one of the first "urban infill" campuses in the country, consolidates all functions (previously scattered in leased locations) into a single building. Under Chin, the design team inserted a multi-level

Atrium "quad," Berkeley City College (formerly Vista College), 2006

atrium—a vertical "quad"—at the building's core to serve the five thousand students who will use the facility. The canted and curved forms of the concrete and glass structure, Ratcliff's most important building in downtown Berkeley in eighty years, rise in counterpoint to the brick and terra-cotta tower of Walter Ratcliff's 1927 Chamber of Commerce Building at the other end of the block.

HEALTH care and academic work accounted for over 90 percent of Ratcliff's revenues by the 1990s. The diversity of projects, public and private, that characterized the firm in the 1970s and 1980s had been in large part

due to the older principals, whose cultivation of clients waned as retirement approached. Yet the company did not cease offering its services for other kinds of work, and in these smaller jobs, questions of style often drew a more playful and relaxed response than that demanded by institutional work.

With the exception of several small projects in Berkeley, such as the 1993 makeover of a warehouse into bright retail and office space, commercial work ceased. One public commission of note was the 1994 Emeryville Post Office, a striking design by the talented Kava Massih. Two housing complexes undertaken for Sunrise Assisted Living, in Oakland and Walnut Creek, provided homelike settings for seniors. And Pam Helmich brought in one major preservation project with the merger: the award-winning rehabilitation of the 1896 Alameda City Hall, an East Bay landmark ranking among California's oldest functioning civic structures.

Ratcliff did persist in one area of specialization, the planning and design of public and private K–12 schools, carving out a niche that seems likely to endure. Though the contracts were relatively modest, the intangible rewards of community involvement were substantial. Under the direction of Dan Wetherell, these projects imparted a sense of continuity, building on a Ratcliff tradition extending back to the early years of the practice.

Alameda City Hall, 1997. The rehabilitation of this 1896 landmark (by the San Francisco firm of Percy & Hamilton) included the restoration of the lobby, which had been marred by an elevator addition in the central stairway arch.

U.S. Post Office, Emeryville, 1994. Kava Massih's design employed industrial materials and motifs, such as the monitor-like windows, as well as stuck-on programmatic elements, such as the stucco bathroom block (left). "I wanted to create the look of a building that had grown over time," he says. "Like the factories and warehouses of the setting."

Prospect Sierra School, El Cerrito, 2003. The new library and
administration wing is a component of Ratcliff's master plan for
this two-campus private school.

In the case of Head-Royce School, in the Oakland hills, the historical associations were palpable—Walter Ratcliff had designed a number of buildings for the Arts and Crafts campus of its Berkeley predecessor, Anna Head School.[10] For the Oakland campus, the firm produced a master plan and three new structures—a lower school (K–5), middle school (6–8), and gymnasium—opened in the 1990s. The board-and-batten aesthetic of the classroom buildings responded to community requests while referring to the architectural traditions of the old campus.

The firm's most distinguished school of the decade was Rosa Parks Elementary, in Berkeley. Completed in 1997, the award-winning project epitomized careful planning translated into design. In response to citizen concerns about the facility fitting into its residential setting—and also functioning as a "beacon" that offered preschool, child care, health care, and other programs—the design team (Kava Massih, Christie Coffin, and Don Kasamoto) created a village-like cluster of angled and gabled forms enhanced by bold colors, simultaneously reflecting and commenting on the historic Berkeley neighborhood at its doorstep.

Two small schools of the new century, both completed in 2002, demonstrate responsiveness to the natural and historical dimensions of site. In its plan for Seven Hills School, on a rural hillside in suburban Walnut Creek, barns and other existing structures were accommodated and indoor-outdoor spaces were linked and oriented to the sun and view. New buildings were designed to reflect the barn vernacular, with open-truss interiors evoking an earlier Ratcliff tradition as well.

Blue Oak School, in Napa, brought the firm full circle, incorporating rehabilitation, contextualism, and sustainability. The original school, built in 1909 in a Mission Revival/Arts and Crafts mode, had been modernized and converted to offices in the 1950s, and abandoned in the 1990s. The rehabilitation retained significant features and restored others, with added amenities, and the new library/multi-purpose building displayed harmonious styling. The environmentally friendly and nontoxic materials included recyclable carpets, wall fabrics of recycled polyester, and cork floors replacing wood where appropriate.

The most innovative component of Blue Oak is its heating and cooling system. "A geothermal ground source HVAC system provides heating and air conditioning," a company brochure explains. "This system collects the earth's natural heat in winter through a series of pipes; fluid circulating in the loops carries heat to the building in winter and to the ground in the summer." In the words of Dan Wetherell, "Blue Oak School is environmentally smart. It is the first independent lower school in California to install a geo-exchange heating and cooling system to reduce energy consumption. From the aesthetic effort

Blue Oak School, Napa, 2002. The staircase in the renovated school building retains its original wood landing and stairs, with harmonious new balusters, newels, and handrails. The new skylight provides natural illumination.

Rosa Parks Elementary School, Allston Way, Berkeley,
1997. The design team conceived of the school as a miniature
neighborhood of homelike structures and introduced bright,
optimistic colors at the clients' request.

to sustain the historic fabric of downtown Napa by recycling an old schoolhouse to the budgetary emphasis on employing green materials, Blue Oak School is a model of sustainability."

THIS "model of sustainability" incorporates core concerns—preservation, conservation, and respect for nature—in the century-long practice of architecture at the Ratcliff office. Green architecture is a contemporary analogue of the Arts and Crafts movement; it is that sensibility in twenty-first-century mode.

For Walter Ratcliff, Jr., and his son Robert Ratcliff, that sensibility meant designing buildings with a fine attention to materials and a high regard for site; for Kit Ratcliff's generation, it has meant responsible design—survival—in a depleted and threatened environment. The existing urban fabric, the materials used in construction, the energy used to heat and cool the building: such concerns are more germane to current affairs than the rustic imagery of the Bay Tradition, though both flow from the same source.[11]

Ratcliff's most lauded contribution to sustainable design is the Green Matrix (www.greenmatrix.net), a website used on a daily basis by architects and clients worldwide. It is the first website to cross-reference standard phases of project design, from master planning to post-occupancy, with sustainable topics such as site, water, energy, materials, and indoor environment. A visitor in search of water-saving strategies, for example, would click on the intersection of "master planning" and "water," leading to a page with specific strategies as well as additional resource links.

Green Matrix grew organically in a company culture devoted to shared innovation and sustainable design. It began as a workstation poster containing a simple matrix of topics and phases. Increased input led to a digital database that was transferred to a CD-ROM format. Kit Ratcliff committed the firm to upgrading the database and moving it to the Internet, which took place in the spring of 2004. Green Matrix continues to be offered at no charge to users, providing an instant portal to sustainability for anyone on the planet.

In the firm's recent Berkeley City College project, sustainable building practices and management techniques were brought to the fore in a concerted effort to enhance air quality, conserve energy, provide maximum natural and low-impact lighting, and promote the use of environmentally sensitive materials. The project hopes to secure a U.S. Green Building Council LEED (Leadership in Energy and Environmental Design) rating, the first in Berkeley.

In its commitment to sustainability, as much as in its health care and academic practices, planning, design, and consulting services, and culture of encouragement and respect, the company continues to build the future on the foundation of the past. Ratcliff, at 100, is alive.

TOP: *The principals of Ratcliff: from left, Crodd Chin, Kit Ratcliff, Dan Wetherell, Carolyn Silk, Gary Burk, Roger Hay, David Dersch.* BOTTOM: *The associate principals of Ratcliff: from left, Steve McCollom, Peter Tsugawa, Linda Mahle, Bill Blessing, Bill Wong, Cheryl Lentini, Tom Patterson.*

Coda Yesterday and Tomorrow

A GAP EXISTS between architecture as it is commonly practiced and commonly perceived. To most observers it is about style, and high style at that: photogenic buildings that produce the frissons sought by consumers in a market-driven culture. Visual clamor is a kind of hunger, a cry for recognition.

The serious business of architecture is something else. In the Bay Area, it is a profession practiced by hundreds of firms harnessing the energy of thousands of highly trained and mostly anonymous individuals. They turn out countless designs of technical sophistication, adept planning, and visual strength—buildings of firmness and commodity, if not delight.

Ratcliff is in a class by itself among the architectural firms of the Bay Area: a company that has continued to adapt and grow after a century of unremitting change. The firm has responded to fluctuations of war and peace, ridden out cycles of depression and prosperity, and reinvented itself at critical junctures. It has remained open to new categories of client, new areas of practice, and new types of technology. It is, in short, a living company, and it has outlasted all others of its kind in the Bay Area.

If Ratcliff's defining characteristic—the key to its longevity—is adaptation, the corollary to this is innovation. In three generations of family leadership, the firm has repeatedly shown its willingness to head in new directions. The first building with a steel frame or elevator; the first concert hall or skyscraper; the first hospital or airport terminal; the first solar or geothermal heating system: initial steps such as these have led the firm down a path of continued exploration, discovery, and renewal.

Central to this endeavor has been a sharpened

focus on the people involved in every aspect of the design process. The firm's self-avowed core values emphasize the well-being of its workforce, and this concern remains a distinctive trait of the company culture. Priority is placed on personal growth and success, on open dialogue, on mutual respect, on teambuilding and longevity. As you talk to individuals who work at the firm, it becomes clear that these core values are what the company is primarily about: how it treats people.

Under Walter Ratcliff, the firm was a sole proprietorship with a single voice; under Robert Ratcliff, it became a partnership of several voices; under Kit Ratcliff, the voices have grown in number and in kind—a corporate conversation in which all are invited to have their say: an attempt to place consensus above hierarchy.

And if Walter and Robert Ratcliff gave their clients what they asked for, the firm's approach under Kit Ratcliff has been to ask what it is they truly want. Architect and client enter into a collaborative process of discovery, co-creators of solutions that are at once logically sound and intuitively resonant.

Ratcliff retains a strong sense of its own identity, rooted in the continuities of its history. The weight of that legacy rests on the shoulders of the inheritor; like his father and grandfather before him, he is simultaneously grounded in the physical realm of architecture and animated by the metaphysics of ideas. His thoughts, like theirs, have helped shape the firm's discourse with the world.

Walter Ratcliff spoke the universal, eclectic language of his age, finding in history the vocabulary

to suit his temperament and times. Robert Ratcliff turned to the future, speaking the newly universal language of modernism. Kit Ratcliff inherited the self-reflective perspective of postmodernity, and the language he speaks is at once more localized and more inclusive.

How will Ratcliff choose to address the world as it makes its way through its second century? It is a question worth asking. The firm's expression of an idea has always been an exercise in intelligibility: if we listen, we will hear a cultivated language, spoken with clarity, in a voice of quiet authority.

BERKELEY is another touchstone of the company's meaning. It is the city where the firm had its office and where most of its projects were built during the first half-century of its existence. Berkeley has thrived as a nexus of communities: an interweaving of academic, artistic, business, professional, philosophical, and religious alliances.

It is also one of those rare places that have given rise to architecture of the highest order. This was due largely to the presence of the University of California and its School of Architecture. With a lineage extending from Maybeck and Howard to Wurster and Esherick, Moore and Alexander, and beyond, Berkeley has reflected and influenced American architecture through the eras of historicism and modernism to the postmodern present.

To begin with Maybeck and Howard is to point to the influence of the Ecole des Beaux-Arts in the formation of a tradition of sophisticated historicist design in San Francisco Bay Area architecture and planning from the closing years of the nineteenth century to World War II. This is the milieu that formed Walter H. Ratcliff, Jr., and his essays in eclecticism were in the mainstream of professional practice during the peak period of his career.

To cite Wurster and Esherick is to invoke the place of modernism in Bay Area architecture, which by World War II had supplanted historicism as the dominant language of the design professions. Robert Ratcliff, a contemporary of Esherick, was part of that heroic generation that believed in the potential of modern architecture to reform society.

The mention of Moore and Alexander hints at the complexity of the postmodern discourse, the ongoing search for an architecture that is responsive to human needs, holistically open to the global legacy of the built environment, and attentive to nature in all the associations of that word. This is the world of Kit Ratcliff.

IT IS NOT surprising that a feeling for nature has colored the work of the firm since the beginning. The Ratcliff family arrived in Berkeley as the local Arts and Crafts community was taking root, and the Reverend Walter Henry Ratcliff was likely steeped in that tradition. In California in the 1890s, Berkeley contained the new spirit in most concentrated fashion, and in Berkeley it would never die.

Raised in a family pervaded by the yearnings of the Arts and Crafts movement, Walter Harris Ratcliff came to adulthood in a town that was by then the center of the movement in the western United States. His shingled houses set in gardens were clearly in that tradition, while his later revivalist residences often shared in that sensibility by their careful attention to materials, workmanship, and landscaping.

Robert Ratcliff clearly showed his receptivity to the evolving Arts and Crafts movement—which after World War II acquired its own regional label, as the Bay Tradition—in his modern houses of the 1940s and 1950s. An inflationary rise in the cost of building materials, as well as the depletion of the forests themselves, meant that Berkeley's wood aesthetic—spanning three-quarters of a century, from Maybeck in the 1890s to Moore in the 1960s—was no longer sustainable.

At this juncture in regional (and world) history, the Arts and Crafts impulse underwent another transmutation. No longer a set of images composed of rustic materials and vernacular precedents, though such motifs have persisted, it became instead a search for sustainable design. Green architecture, so-called, is driven not by formal questions of image and allusion but by deeper issues of survival. Sustainability imbues the thinking of Kit Ratcliff, not as a designer so much as a senior partner—an architect provocateur living out his Berkeley legacy.

NOR IS IT surprising that the firm has continually branched out into new areas of practice over the past century. The ambitious, entrepreneurial spirit of Walter H. Ratcliff, Jr., compelled him to work with all kinds of clients—and he didn't wait for them to come to the office, he went and found them. His practice is a textbook case of diversification, from his early emphasis on residential design to his ever-expanding portfolio of building types: apartment building, club, church, seminary, academic hall, dormitory, bank, showroom, sky-scraper. He was willing, and able, to design just about anything.

The same held true for Robert, who transformed the company in every conceivable way: aesthetically, procedurally, and programmatically. The new modernist idiom of the buildings by Ratcliff, Slama & Cadwalader could not have provided a more vivid contrast with the historicist buildings of Walter H. Ratcliff, Jr. But that is not really the point. The same innovative spirit was at work in the son as in the father; his openness to change was identical. He partnered with other firms and took on unprecedented jobs—shopping center, parking structure, hospital—leading to new areas of practice.

With Kit Ratcliff, the same is also true. Like his father and grandfather, he has not hesitated to embrace the challenges of any job—an airport terminal, an out-of-state campus complex, ever-larger academic and health care facilities, or the requirements of small, intimate schools. Under his guidance, and that of his partners, the seventy-five people who today comprise Ratcliff are prepared, in a paraphrase of the firm's "core purpose," to work with people through architecture to evoke new worlds.

Where will the company go next? What new areas will be tried? How many people will come away from those encounters with a new understanding of themselves and of the worlds they have created together?

Notes

Chapter 1

1. Though he did not share his father's middle name, Walter H(arris) Ratcliff would append a "Jr." at the outset of his architectural career to distinguish himself from his father, who was well known in Berkeley circles.

2. See Richard Longstreth, *On the Edge of the World* (New York: The Architectural History Foundation; Cambridge, Mass., and London: MIT Press, 1983), chapter 1: "Academic Eclecticism: The Question of Style." McKim, Mead & White were the foremost exponents of Beaux-Arts classicism derived from Renaissance sources; Richardson developed a more personal style based on the medieval Romanesque. The Beaux-Arts-inspired classicism of the so-called "American Renaissance" achieved forceful expression at the 1893 World's Columbian Exposition in Chicago, a hugely popular venue that inspired the City Beautiful movement in American cities.

3. Genealogical information is provided by Kenneth E. Ratcliff, *My Descendant Chart,* a well-researched family tree that includes dates and places of births, deaths, and marriages of family members back to the late eighteenth century. The compiler is a great-grandson of Walter Henry Ratcliff.

4. This figure is based on anecdotal family lore; it would have been a substantial sum, equivalent to at least $100,000 in today's U.S. currency.

5. The choice of Redcliffe Square seems more than coincidence. According to one account of the Ratcliff name, whose lineage in Britain extends back to the Norman Conquest, a twelfth-century knight named Nicholas FitzGilbert de Tailbois established a manor near Radcliffe, a Lancashire river-town named for its red cliffs. The family became known as "de Radcliffe," later shortened to "Radcliffe," one of the variant spellings being "Ratcliff." See Clarence Earl Ratcliff, *Richard Ratcliff of Lancashire, England, and Talbot County, Maryland, and His Ancestors and Descendents, 1066–1988* (1988; rev. 1994). This out-of-print book can be read on the website "The Ratcliff Family Tree."

6. See Robert W. Ratcliff, *The Ratcliff Architects, in Berkeley Since 1909,* volume I, an oral history conducted in 1989 by Suzanne B. Riess, Regional Oral History Office, The Bancroft Library, University of California, Berkeley, 1990. Unless otherwise noted, all quotes by Robert Ratcliff are from this oral history.

7. *The Simple Home* was dedicated to Bernard Maybeck, who designed Keeler's Northside residence in 1895—the architect's first house commission.

8. The house, at 1643 Euclid Avenue, was designed by Walter H. Ratcliff, Jr., while a student at the

university. See *Edwards Transcript of Records,* 30 Apr. 1902. The house burned in the 1923 Berkeley fire.

9. Ratcliff served briefly as rector of the Church of the Good Shepherd, at Hearst Avenue and Ninth Street in west Berkeley, and was also associated with the Church of the Advent, in San Francisco. Good Shepherd's members included the educator Anna Head; built in 1878, it is Berkeley's oldest surviving church building.

10. Originally located in San Francisco, the seminary moved to Berkeley in 1901 to establish closer ties with the university. In 1916, the name was changed to the Pacific School of Religion to reflect its ecumenical spirit.

11. William Frederic Badè, *The Life and Letters of John Muir* (1924), 1:209. Quoted in Leslie Mandelson Freudenheim and Elisabeth Sacks Sussman, *Building with Nature* (Santa Barbara and Salt Lake City: Peregrine Smith, Inc., 1974), p. 10.

12. "Romance of Mountain Climbers Culminates in Marriage," *San Francisco Call,* 27 Sept. 1906. One of Walter Ratcliff's early commissions was a South-side house for his sister and brother-in-law, discussed (and illustrated) in chapter 2.

13. "College Sorority Girls Tell Their Engagements," *San Francisco Call,* 25 Nov. 1910. Ethel was a tennis champion at the University of California. She and Martin made regular visits to California as late as the 1960s, keeping alive the connection between the two branches of the family. They had three children.

14. Though his eyesight recovered, all of the teeth in his lower jaw had to be removed.

15. Maybeck taught courses in architectural drawing at the University of California when Ratcliff was a student, but there is no evidence that he attended these classes. The school of architecture was not established until 1903.

16. *Edwards Transcript of Records,* 2 Aug. 1901; 30 Apr. 1902. The contractor in 1901 was I. W. Bridenbecker; built for $1,820, the house still stands at 2611 Parker Street. The 1902 family residence was built by R. R. Bixby for $3,700. Ratcliff designed at least five other speculative houses in Berkeley for his family, between 1904 and 1909.

17. *Edwards Transcript of Records,* 23 Dec. 1901. The contractor was Bridenbecker; the cost, $2,060. Much altered, the house still stands on Martin Luther King, Jr., Way. Robert Ratcliff recollected that his father had designed "four or five" houses for McFarland when he was a student; this is the only one that has been documented. McFarland commissioned six other speculative houses in Berkeley in 1902; the published contract notices state "plans by owner," an ambiguous phrase that could mean either that the owner produced the plans himself or procured them from someone else. They are quite possibly the work of young Ratcliff. Built in rows of three, at 1929, 1933, and 1935 Virginia Street, and 1911, 1915, and 1917 Vine Street, the two-story, central-hall houses are quite similar (some are identical): Colonial Revival boxes with hip roofs, side porches, and cladding of horizontal wood siding or shingles. Bridenbecker & Gray built them at a cost of $1,449 each. *Edwards Transcript of Records,* 14 Apr. and 23 Apr. 1902. Ratcliff would design three speculative houses in Berkeley for McFarland in 1906, including one with himself as co-owner; after opening his own office he would design many more. Biographical information on the McFarland family is from the U.S. Census (1910, 1920, 1930) and from obituaries of Joseph L. McFarland ("J. L. M'Farland, Financier, Dies" and "Funeral Services for J. L. M'Farland," *Berkeley Daily Gazette,*" 11 Oct. 1922 and 12 Oct. 1922) and Charles L. McFarland

("Building, Loan Official Dies," *Berkeley Daily Gazette,* 8 Mar. 1940).

18. The closest parallel from the period was the Chicago suburb of Oak Park, with its own resident genius, Frank Lloyd Wright.

19. According to *Architect and Engineer* (Oct. 1914, p. 58), "when Architect Henry A. Schulze was in active practice, Mr. Ratcliff was a member of his working staff." Schulze was a long-established San Francisco architect who moved his office to Oakland in 1909 and retired soon after. It is not known when Ratcliff worked for him, though the tenure was probably brief.

20. John Galen Howard imposed his own Beaux-Arts vision on the Berkeley campus, modifying Bénard's plan as well as designing all of the new campus buildings. His first residence, which he designed, was built in 1903 at 2421 Ridge Road, overlooking the campus. Like the nearby Ratcliff residence, it burned in the 1923 fire; the site now forms part of the Church Divinity School of the Pacific. See Sally B. Woodbridge, *John Galen Howard and the University of California* (Berkeley, Los Angeles, and London: University of California Press, 2002), pp. 69–73.

21. Quoted in Woodbridge, *John Galen Howard,* pp. 90–92.

22. Howard's office was in downtown Berkeley from 1902 to 1905, when it moved to San Francisco. Howard "petitioned the regents . . . for authorization to open an office in San Francisco, where, he argued, qualified assistants, contractors, and materials were more available and less costly." Woodbridge, *John Galen Howard,* p. 90.

23. The British School in Rome occupied the Palazzo Odescalchi until 1916, when it moved into a neoclassical edifice designed by Edward Lutyens. The school remains in operation as a center of research focusing on the archeology, history, and culture of Italy, as well as on contemporary art and architecture.

Chapter 2

1. Michael R. Corbett, *Splendid Survivors* (San Francisco: California Living Books, 1979) remains the most cogent overview of downtown San Francisco's historical and architectural development. One building survives from the Panama-Pacific International Exposition: Maybeck's Palace of Fine Arts, reconstructed in the 1960s with permanent materials.

2. Steam trains, beginning in 1876, and electric streetcars, in 1891, connected Berkeley with ferry terminals in Oakland, but the new electrified systems expedited the commute. The Key Route consolidated independent lines, upgraded equipment, and opened a new ferry pier closer to Berkeley—in Emeryville, on the site of the east end of the Bay Bridge.

3. "In the months following the 1906 earthquake about 20,000 San Franciscans moved permanently to Berkeley." Susan Dinkelspiel Cerny, *Berkeley Landmarks* (Berkeley: Berkeley Architectural Heritage Association, 2001), p. 86.

4. The leading architects, including Maybeck, Howard, and Morgan, had offices in San Francisco, the region's professional center. Ratcliff & Jacobs was at 20 Montgomery Street, in the Union Trust Company Building, a fashionable address on the architecturally impressive intersection of Post, Montgomery, and Market Streets. The building was demolished in the 1960s to make way for the Wells Fargo Building. See Corbett, *Splendid Survivors,* p. 46, for historic views.

5. Located at 2624 Hillegass Avenue, in the Southside, the clubhouse was vacated in 1917, when

the tennis club moved to its current site near the Claremont Hotel. Converted to residential use in 1920, the old clubhouse was designated a Berkeley City Landmark in 1989. See Cerny, *Berkeley Landmarks,* pp. 224–225.

6. Alfred Henry Jacobs (1882–1954) would become one of San Francisco's best-known Jewish architects. His work in the city included the Herald Hotel (1910), California Theater (1917), Congregation Emanu-El Religious School (1918), Pacific Hebrew Orphan Asylum (1921), Granada Theater (1921), and Curran Theater (1922). He also designed the whimsical Winema Theater (1920), a rustic redwood temple with columns of unpeeled logs, in the northern California lumber town of Scotia, and the standardized white storefront still used by See's Candies. Aaron T. Kornblum, "Chronology of Important Dates in the Life of Alfred Henry Jacobs" (Berkeley: Western Jewish History Center, Judah L. Magnes Museum, ms., n.d. [2004]).

7. The First National Bank Building stood at the southwest corner of Shattuck Avenue and Center Street. It was demolished in the 1960s for the twelve-story Great Western Building (1970), the city's tallest off-campus structure.

8. Tallies are based on buildings that have been documented by research; the actual figures are probably higher. By 1916, for example, contract numbers on Ratcliff's blueprints reached No. 250, compared to about 150 documented buildings for the same period. The percentage of speculative houses Ratcliff designed for investors may also be higher, since the names of many one-time clients do not show up in city directories at those addresses.

9. In an essay in a Northbrae house-tour booklet, Trish Hawthorne notes that "no house could cost less than $2,500," and that "Mason-McDuffie retained Walter Ratcliff to assist buyers with house plans." See Berkeley Architectural Heritage Association, *Northbrae* (Berkeley: BAHA, 1994). Mason-McDuffie's principal subdivision outside Berkeley was St. Francis Wood in San Francisco, begun in 1912. Gutterson would serve as supervising architect, designing nearly a fifth of the subdivision's 550 residences over four decades. Ratcliff designed one residence in St. Francis Wood, in 1913, his only known house in San Francisco following the breakup of his partnership with Jacobs. See Cerny, "Henry Gutterson," in *Toward a Simpler Way of Life* (Berkeley, Los Angeles, London: University of California Press, 1997). Cerny, *Berkeley Landmarks,* includes overviews of McDuffie and the Claremont and Northbrae tracts.

10. Alameda County Home Builders, Inc., occupied Room 207, later moving to Room 222 of the First National Bank Building. The company was incorporated in Berkeley on Nov. 27, 1911, with authorized capital stock in the amount of $75,000. The directors were identified as Walter H. Ratcliff, Jr., Charles L. McFarland, W. Henry Ratcliff, and Joseph L. McFarland. *Articles of Incorporation of Alameda County Home Builders Inc.* (Sacramento: Office of the Secretary of State, State of California, filed Dec. 1, 1911). McFarland commissioned approximately thirty houses from Ratcliff between December 1908 and January 1916, evenly divided between contracts under his own name (1908 to 1911) and Alameda County Home Builders (1912 to 1916). With the exception of a few bungalows built in Oakland, all of the houses were located in Berkeley. During these same years, Alameda County Home Builders also built two fraternity houses and a small apartment house in Berkeley. It is not known to what degree Ratcliff invested

in the houses commissioned by McFarland prior to 1912; family memory suggests that the two men had a profit-sharing arrangement dating back to their first project in 1901.

11. Published contract notices from 1901 to 1916 provide construction costs for some of Ratcliff's houses. Speculative houses ranged from about $2,000 for bungalows and cheap two-story houses to about $4,000 for more substantial two-story dwellings. Contract amounts for owner-occupied houses were typically in the $3,500 to $10,000 range; very few cost more. Inflation should be taken into account when comparing the costs of earlier and later houses.

12. Located at 2799 Benvenue Avenue, this was the first Berkeley residence of Charles McFarland and his parents, Joseph and Mary McFarland. In 1908, the family moved into a new house, with bay view, at 2360 Prospect Street (designed by Ratcliff & Jacobs). This became their permanent residence. Both buildings survive, though the house on Prospect is greatly altered.

13. The 1908 house for his sister, at 97 Parkside Drive, was Ratcliff's first commission in Claremont. The 1912 house for McFarland is at 43 Parkside Drive.

14. *Daily Pacific Builder,* 24 Apr. 1911. These bungalows, each of which cost $2,000 to build, are located at 256, 260, and 266 38th Street, near the Kaiser Medical Center. Ratcliff designed approximately three dozen bungalows over the course of his career; most were built in Oakland.

15. Ratcliff likely designed the Mead house in the fall of 1903, soon after he went to work for Howard; it is his earliest known residence for someone other than his parents or McFarland. The contract notice, listing a cost of $2,520, appeared in *Daily Pacific Builder* on 28 Dec. 1903; the notice of completion was published 14 Apr. 1904. The Mead house,

2842 Hillegass Avenue, and Badè house, 2616 College Avenue, are extant but altered.

16. The house in Claremont, at 195 The Uplands, was Ratcliff's first job for McFarland after parting ways with Jacobs; it was his second commission in Claremont. A contract notice appeared in *Daily Pacific Builder* on 29 Dec. 1908. The building permit for the Buckman residence, 920 Shattuck Avenue, was issued on 20 May 1909. One of the first houses in Northbrae, it was designated a Berkeley City Landmark in 1994. Elmer Buckman was president of the Keystone Construction Company. See Cerny, *Berkeley Landmarks,* p. 270.

17. Widespread in medieval and late-medieval England and northern Europe, where wood was plentiful, half-timbering utilized a structural framework of hand-hewn timbers with infill of wattle and daub. Revivalist half-timbering was often associated with Tudor England, hence the term "Tudor Revival."

18. Founded in Berkeley in 1887 as a day and boarding school for grades one to twelve, the Anna Head School for Girls moved to a site two blocks south of the university campus, between Channing Way and Haste Street, in 1892. The campus, acquired by the University of California in 1964, remains a notable Arts and Crafts ensemble. The original 1892 building, designed by Soule Edgar Fisher (Anna Head's cousin), is widely considered the first shingled building in Berkeley. Ratcliff designed nine shingled buildings and additions between 1911 and 1927. The school was listed on the National Register of Historic Places in 1980, and designated a city landmark in 1981. See Cerny, *Berkeley Landmarks,* pp. 189–190.

19. *Building and Industrial News,* 11 July 1911. This was Ratcliff's first published work; a photograph of the house and garden appeared in the April 1913 issue

of *Architect and Engineer.* The house still stands at 2730 Belrose Avenue, but the garden has been built over. It was Anna Head who introduced Walter Ratcliff to his future wife, Muriel Williams.

20. *Building and Industrial News,* 2 July 1912. The house, which stood at 130 King Avenue, northeast corner of Farrugut Avenue, is no longer extant; the site has been redeveloped. Arthur H. Breed (1865–1953) sat in the California state senate from 1913 to 1935, serving as president pro tem after 1917. Among his legislative actions was helping to formulate and pass the 1919 California Real Estate Act, which set licensing standards for realtors. "The History of the Oakland Association of Realtors" (oar.org). Ratcliff's oldest surviving residential design displaying stucco-and-tile classicism is the 1909 Montgomery house, 45 Oakridge Road, in Berkeley's Claremont district.

21. Now a fraternity house with a modern addition and minus the terrace garden, the former Shearman residence stands at the northeast corner of Piedmont Avenue and Dwight Way. A drawn-out design process is inferred from the appearance in the *Daily Pacific Builder* of separate contract notices in May 1913 and Oct. 1913.

22. This was Maybeck's second residence, built in 1909 at 2701 Buena Vista Way; it burned in the 1923 fire. The Ratcliff and Maybeck families had become friends through the Hillside Club, and Walter knew the Maybeck home well. Robert recalled that his father "admired Maybeck, but felt that he was not a practical man . . . He told me that a lot of times he wrote agreements for Maybeck. Mrs. Maybeck would bring down papers and say, 'Do you think this is the way it should be?' He'd go through them . . . and then she'd be satisfied."

23. Also destroyed in the 1923 fire, the house would have been familiar to Ratcliff, since Howard entertained his office staff there frequently. The plan and several early views are in Woodbridge, *John Galen Howard,* pp. 69–72.

24. Two contract notices that probably refer to this house appeared in *Daily Pacific Builder,* on 18 Apr. and 19 Apr. 1914, with the cost of construction listed as $4,072 and $8,000, respectively. The house would be enlarged in 1923 by extending the rear wing to create two more bedrooms. The bay windows in the living room were also added at that time. The builder, Walter Sorenson, was the contractor for many of Ratcliff's buildings.

25. A contract notice for the Nickerson residence, 200 Tunnel Road, appeared in *Daily Pacific Builder* on 18 Apr. 1914. The listed construction cost of $23,063 was second only to the Breed mansion among Ratcliff's pre–World War I houses.

26. Charles Peter Weeks won the competition, which carried a cash prize of $5,000. The ten second-place winners each received $1,000. Along with Ratcliff, they included Charles W. Dickey, John J. Donovan, William Mooser, and O'Brien & Werner. "Result of the Alameda County Infirmary Competition," *Architect and Engineer,* June 1913. See also Charles Peter Weeks, "How the Alameda Hospital Competition Was Won," *Architect and Engineer,* Aug. 1913. Weeks's scheme remained largely unrealized. After 1917, the infirmary was rebuilt by the county architect, Henry H. Meyers, who also designed Highland Hospital; when Highland opened in 1926, the Alameda County Infirmary was renamed Fairmont Hospital.

27. City directories list Masten and Hurd in Ratcliff's office in the years 1913 to 1917. Yelland's connection with the firm during this same period is cited in Lauren Weiss Bricker, "William Raymond Yelland," in *Toward a Simpler Way of Life.* Charles F. Masten (1886–1973) graduated from UC Berkeley

in 1912. Lester W. Hurd (1894–1967) was a 1912 graduate of Berkeley High School. They did not attend architecture school, instead receiving their training in Ratcliff's office; Masten received his license in 1914 (reissued 1920), Masten in 1922. Around 1924 they formed a versatile partnership, Masten & Hurd, with offices in San Francisco until the late 1960s. William Raymond Yelland (1890–1966) received a B.S. in architecture from UC Berkeley in 1913. He opened an office in Oakland in 1924, becoming a noted designer of Period Revival houses.

28. A church bulletin in a Ratcliff family scrapbook includes a picture of Mission of the Good Samaritan along with a short history citing Ratcliff as the architect. The building is no longer standing; the site, at Oak and Ninth Streets, is now adjoined by the Oakland Museum and Laney College. St. Peter's Church is at Broadway and Lawton Avenue; the parish hall is intact. *Building and Engineering News,* 18 Feb. 1914. The San Francisco parish hall was built in 1910 for the Church of the Advent, on Fell Street, where Ratcliff's father sometimes officiated. *Edwards Transcript of Records,* 6 Aug. 1910.

29. A building permit for the Glen Garry was issued in May 1912 to P. George Gow, a mining engineer who had previously commissioned a speculative house from Ratcliff; the listed cost of construction was $28,542. Spared by the 1923 fire, the building stood at the southwest corner of Ridge Road and LeRoy Avenue, across from Cloyne Court. Along with other buildings on the block, it was razed for Etcheverry Hall (Skidmore, Owings & Merrill, 1964), the first extension of the UC College of Engineering into the Northside. Soda Hall, which houses the College of Engineering's Computer Science Division, was built on an adjoining site in the 1990s.

30. A tour booklet by the Berkeley Architectural Heritage Association says of the Channing: "This is certainly one of Berkeley's most beautiful apartment houses, and one of Walter Ratcliff's best designs." *Frederick Law Olmsted's Berkeley Legacy— Piedmont Way and the Berkeley Property Tract* (BAHA, 1995). Located in the Southside at 2409 College Avenue, the Channing was developed by the Alameda County Home Investment Co., a firm in which McFarland and Ratcliff had an interest. The company was incorporated in Berkeley in 1912 with five coequal shareholders and directors— C. L. McFarland, J. L. McFarland, W. H. Ratcliff, Jr., J. M. Wiley, and S. S. Quackenbush. *Articles of Incorporation of Alameda County Home Investment Co.* (Sacramento: Office of the Secretary of State, State of California, filed Sept. 27, 1912). This company, like Alameda County Home Builders, Inc., was formed for the purpose of entering into a wide range of real estate and construction activities, but its only known venture was the Channing. The building permit for the $30,000 structure was issued April 9, 1913. The building's stucco-and-tile palette bears comparison to Ratcliff's three-story, six-unit Waste and Clark Apartments, 2126 Bancroft Way, also built in 1913.

31. *Daily Pacific Builder,* 8 Jan., 27 Jan., 3 Mar., 30 Apr. 1914. Located at 2500 Telegraph Avenue, corner of Durant, the Cambridge was touted in the 1915 Polk-Husted Directory: "Two, three, and four-room apartments and single rooms, completely furnished, thoroughly modern elevator service; open Jan. 1915." The building's principal owner was the prominent Berkeley attorney J. A. Elston, who was elected to Congress in 1914. An 1897 graduate of the University of California, Elston was married to the granddaughter of John LeConte, the first professor of physics and third president of the

university. Elston's firm, Elston, Clark & Nichols, was located on the second floor of the First National Bank Building, and one of his corporate clients was Alameda County Home Builders, Inc. Elston resided at the Cambridge. John P. Young, *Journalism in California: Pacific Coast and Exposition Biographies* (San Francisco: Chronicle Publishing Co., 1915; on sfgenealogy.com). Ratcliff also designed a motion-picture theater for Elston—the Majestic—on the adjoining lot at 2510 Durant Avenue; built in 1914, the theater was converted to a cafeteria in 1917. *Daily Pacific Builder,* 22 Sept. 1914; 11 Jan. 1917. The Cambridge still stands, shorn of its cornice; the Majestic is also extant.

32. The world's first reinforced concrete building was built in San Francisco in 1888; the material's demonstrated resistance to fire led to its wide-spread use in the rebuilding of San Francisco after 1906. "After the fire there was immediately a great deal of reinforced concrete construction of whole buildings, and vastly increased use of it in fire-proofing, floor slabs, curtain walls, and foundations." Corbett, *Splendid Survivors,* pp. 57–58.

33. The design competition for the Berkeley Elks Club was held over the summer of 1913; construction began that fall and was completed around a year later. *Daily Pacific Builder,* 30 Sept., 31 Oct. 1913. "Berkeley Elks Lay Cornerstone," *Oakland Tribune,* 1 Jan. 1914. Contract notices for various segments of the work exceeded $70,000; the newspaper article cited a round figure of $100,000. Designated a Berkeley City Landmark in 1991, the building is located at 2018 Allston Way. Cerny, *Berkeley Landmarks,* pp. 104–105.

34. B. J. S. Cahill, "New Home of the San Francisco Commercial Club," *Architect and Engineer,* Feb. 1916; "San Francisco Commercial [Club] a Big Organization," *San Francisco Chronicle,* 16 Jan. 1916. Estab-lished in 1887 as the Merchants' Club, the organization leased various downtown locations before moving to its new quarters in the Merchants' Exchange Building. The newspaper article cited a total cost of $130,000, including furnishings. Located at 465 California Street, the 1903 Merchants' Exchange Building was the work of the Chicago firm D. H. Burnham and Co., with Willis Polk. It was one of the city's early skyscrapers, and one of the few downtown buildings to survive the earthquake and fire. From 1907 until her retirement in 1951, Julia Morgan maintained her practice on the thirteenth floor of this building, and the post-fire design of the celebrated ground-floor trading hall is attributed to her. The Commercial Club occupied a portion of the thirteenth floor and all of the fourteenth floor; the thirteenth floor space was shared with Morgan's office and perhaps other tenants. Only a portion of the Commercial Club survives in more or less original condition.

35. Once common, the practice of hiring official city (and county) architects is no longer followed; during Ratcliff's tenure, John J. Donovan and John J. Reid, Jr., held the respective posts in Oakland and San Francisco, and Henry H. Meyers was the architect for Alameda County.

36. *Fifth Annual Report of the Mayor and Councilmen of the City of Berkeley, California, Fiscal Year Ending June 30, 1914,* p. 3.

37. *Daily Pacific Builder,* 17 Mar., 8 Apr., 10 Apr. 1914. The firehouses were as follows: No. 2, Durant Avenue north of Shattuck (downtown); No. 7, Claremont Avenue south of Russell (Claremont); No. 8, Ellis Street north of Alcatraz (Southside); and No. 9, LeRoy Avenue north of Cedar (Northside). The downtown station was built of rein-forced concrete; the other firehouses were wood-frame. Only No. 7 is extant, now altered for commercial use. The corporation yard, at 1326 Allston

Way, was brought to completion in January 1917. Though substantially enlarged over the years, it retains most if not all of the original buildings, which were designed to harmonize with their residential setting. The property was designated a Berkeley City Landmark in 2002.

38. B. J. S. Cahill, "The City of Berkeley's New Public School Buildings," *Architect and Engineer,* May 1916, pp. 47–54. All five schools were designed to allow for future expansion. The other four schools were John Muir, by James W. Plachek; Garfield, by Ernest Coxhead; Luther Burbank, by Walter E. Reed; and Francis Willard, by Hobart & Cheney. John Muir and Garfield still stand, but only John Muir is still in use as a school; the half-timbered ensemble memorialized the great naturalist and conservationist, who died in 1914. Thomas Edison School now serves as the maintenance office of the Berkeley Unified School District. Located at 1720 Oregon Street, it is partially demolished and otherwise altered, though the 1920 gymnasium addition by Ratcliff is intact.

39. Walter H. Ratcliff, Jr., "The Recent Berkeley School Buildings," *Architect and Engineer,* May 1916, pp. 55–63.

40. In 1913, Berkeley, with Oakland, retained Werner Hegemann to prepare a city plan. Shortly after the plan was completed, in 1914, the Berkeley city council appointed a "city-planning committee." The civic art commission was an outgrowth of the committee. The city council also appointed a "building code committee" in 1914, with Ratcliff as a member; the duties of this committee were likewise taken over by the civic art commission. *Seventh Annual Report of the Mayor and Councilmen of the City of Berkeley, California, Fiscal Year Ending June 30, 1916.*

41. Frederick Jennings, "Some Recent Residences and Other Work by Walter H. Ratcliff, Jr.," *Architect and Engineer,* Oct. 1914, pp. 47–67. Ratcliff's quick ascent to professional recognition was underscored by the misspelling of his name in the same magazine a little over a year earlier, in June 1913, when his entry for the new Alameda County Infirmary was attributed to "C. W. Ratcliffe, Jr." Ratcliff would also be published in the magazine *The Architect,* which ran images of several of his houses and Edison School, in 1917 and 1918.

Chapter 3

1. One of the victims of the pandemic was Phoebe Apperson Hearst, who died in 1919, at the age of 77.

2. Tudor revivalism appeared on John Galen Howard's Stephens Hall (1923) and the adjoining Moses Hall (1931) by George W. Kelham. Kelham succeeded Howard as supervising architect after Howard resigned in 1924. Kelham held the position until his death in 1936.

3. "Monument to War Heroes to Be Imposing," *San Francisco Chronicle,* 31 May 1919. The estimated cost was one million dollars. Ratcliff's vision for a war memorial was realized in different form under a state-mandated and county-funded program of the 1920s and 1930s that resulted in ten "veterans memorial" buildings in Alameda County. Designed by the county architect, Henry H. Meyers, they still stand in Oakland, Berkeley, Alameda, Emeryville, Albany, San Leandro, Hayward, Fremont, Pleasanton, and Livermore. The earliest and largest of the group was the Oakland building, erected in 1926 by Lake Merritt.

4. *Edwards Transcript of Records,* 20 Mar. 1918, 25 Aug. 1919; *Daily Pacific Builder,* 20 Aug. 1919; *Architect and Engineer,* Aug. 1919. The three contracts totaled approximately $150,000. The South of Market warehouse, now converted to office lofts, stands at

128 Spear Street. Both office buildings have been demolished and their sites redeveloped with high-rises. 150 California Street, which stood until the 1990s, was included in the downtown survey published in 1979 as *Splendid Survivors.* Its stucco-and-tile styling included arches, pilasters, and a pent roof. Robert Ratcliff, in his oral history, stated that Billings was his father's tennis partner and benefactor for the Commercial Club job. Other biographical information is from the obituary "Billings, Ship Magnate, Dead," *San Francisco Chronicle,* 13 Dec. 1929.

5. "Office of City Architect Is Abolished by Council," *Berkeley Sun & Letter,* 15 Jan. 1921. Ratcliff was the only person ever to hold the office, which was never reinstated. The mayor voted against the motion, considering it "penny wise and pound foolish." In his final report, Ratcliff had noted that his fees from 1917 to 1920 totaled a paltry $586.50, for jobs like park restrooms, automobile sheds, and repairs to City Hall. These fees did not include the school commissions, which came to him through the school board and were not part of his duties as city architect. The new school was Lincoln School, in west Berkeley; built at a cost in excess of $200,000, it was similar in appearance to Edison. Renamed Malcolm X Elementary School, it still stands at 1731 Prince Street, though totally altered and enlarged. *Daily Pacific Builder,* 28 June 1920; City of Berkeley building permit, 25 Aug. 1920. The gymnasium was an addition to Edison School.

6. Elston, Clark & Nichols, Attorneys. *In the Matter of the Application of Alameda County Home Builders, Inc., a corporation, for Change of Name to Fidelity Mortgage Securities Company of California.* Superior Court, County of Alameda, State of California. June 14, 1918. The Fidelity Mortgage Securities Company remained in existence as late as 1940, with the same business address and officers as the Fidelity Guaranty Building and Loan Association.

7. *Articles of Incorporation of Fidelity Guaranty Building and Loan Association* (Sacramento: Office of the Secretary of State, State of California, filed Aug. 21, 1921). Ratcliff and McFarland together were the majority shareholders, each owning slightly more than 25 percent of the shares. The other founding directors were Everett N. Bee, A. Naglee Burk, C. A. Ferrin, John W. Havens, John McCarthy, Joseph L. McFarland, and C. W. Savage; all except Bee and Burk lived in Berkeley. By 1922, F. Linden Naylor, Robert Sibley, and Donald P. Wingate had replaced Burk, Ferrin, and Joseph McFarland (who died that year). Later directors included Oscar T. Barber, Hughbert S. Luce, Lester Hink, Elmer E. Nichols, and A. B. Tanner. *Annual Report on the Building and Loan Associations of the State of California by the Building and Loan Commissioner* (Sacramento: California State Printing Office, 1922–1940, *passim*). Now known as savings and loans, building and loan associations in the United States were the outgrowth of nineteenth-century associations established by working-class people who pooled resources to finance mortgages. *Fidelity Facts,* a quarterly news-letter put out by Fidelity Guaranty, included articles about the origins and operations of the company, e.g., "Fidelity—Its Beginning and Its Progress" (*Fidelity Facts,* Jan. 1930) and "Fidelity—Guaranty Type Association" (*Fidelity Facts,* Apr. 1930).

8. *Building and Engineering News,* 24 Oct. 1925. Located at 2323 Shattuck Avenue, the building was designated a city landmark in 1983. Cerny, *Berkeley Landmarks,* pp. 108–109. The quotation is from the Chamber of Commerce newspaper, *The Courier,* 29 May 1926.

9. The department store closed in 1985, and the space has been reconstructed for offices. See Cerny,

Berkeley Landmarks, pp. 102–104. The largely intact Mason-McDuffie Building, 2101 Shattuck Avenue, was designated a city landmark in 1985. Cerny, *Berkeley Landmarks,* pp. 115–116. Construction began in the fall of 1928. *Daily Pacific Builder,* 25 Sept. 1928. The Berkeley Guarantee Building and Loan Association, founded in 1922 with McDuffie as a director, operated for many years out of this building.

10. Betty Marvin, "Chamber of Commerce Building, Berkeley, California" (Nomination to the National Register of Historic Places, Oct. 1984). The Chamber of Commerce Building "was twice as high as existing buildings and remained the tallest structure until 1970, when the Great Western Building was completed." Cerny, *Berkeley Landmarks,* pp. 124–125. The building commonly went by the name emblazoned on its giant rooftop sign: "American Trust Company." It has been known as the Wells Fargo Bank Building since 1960, when that bank acquired American Trust. Designated a city landmark in 1984, it was listed on the National Register of Historic Places in 1985. The twelve-story Great Western Building, on the other side of Center Street, occupies the site of the First National Bank Building.

11. *The Courier,* 29 Jan. 1927. The respective heights of the Chamber of Commerce Building and the Campanile are 149 feet and 303 feet.

12. Harvey Helfand, *The Campus Guide: University of California, Berkeley* (New York: Princeton Architectural Press, 2002), p. 62. Helfand states that the San Francisco firm of Vickery, Atkins and Torrey worked with Ratcliff on the design of Morrison Library. This firm had supervised the original interior design of Doe Memorial Library. May Treat Morrison also underwrote the Music Department's Morrison Hall (1958), designed by Gardner Dailey. Ratcliff's other important classicist work of the period was the annex to the Mendocino County Courthouse, in Ukiah, completed at the same time as the Morrison Library. Clad in sandstone, with rusticated base, fluted pilasters, and arcaded windows, the two-story Beaux-Arts structure emulated the elegance of seventeenth-century French architecture.

13. A fourth wing, with a much larger hall, was added to the clubhouse in 1924. Since the 1930s, the club has been known as the Mira Vista Country Club. The address is 7901 Cutting Blvd., El Cerrito.

14. Founded in 1962, the Graduate Theological Union (GTU) is the largest consortium of religious schools in the western United States. Its nine members represent Protestant, Catholic, and interdenominational creeds, and its nine affiliates include Jewish, Orthodox Christian, and Buddhist institutes. All but one of the member schools are in Berkeley, and of these, six are grouped together in the Northside. The GTU Library, opened in the 1980s, occupies a hilltop site at Ridge Road and Scenic Avenue, facing both the Pacific School of Religion and the Church Divinity School of the Pacific. "Holy Hill" is a phrase commonly used by Berkeley residents and the media.

15. Perhaps one should not read too much into this. The architect and the trustees were also simply subscribing to revivalist convention, seeking to endow the school with the patina of history.

16. Harland E. Hogue, *Christian Seed in Western Soil: Pacific School of Religion through a Century* (Berkeley: PSR, 1965). Badè, it will be recalled, was Ratcliff's former brother-in-law.

17. "The New Pacific School of Religion," *Boston Evening Transcript,* 25 Mar. 1922, part 4, p. 13.

18. Hearst had commissioned John Galen Howard

to design a residence for the site, but her death in 1919 left the project unbuilt.

19. It is not known to what degree Ratcliff adapted his old design to the new site.

20. "An Impressive Service Marks Library Opening; Confer Honors on Architect Ratcliff at Dedication," *Berkeley Daily Gazette,* 4 Feb. 1926. The newspaper cited "an expenditure of $300,000" for the administration building, library wing, and dormitory, with an estimated cost of $2 million for the entire proposed campus. Ratcliff would design a Spanish revivalist house for Dr. Swartz in Kensington in 1928.

21. The building acquired its present name after the library collection was transferred to the GTU Library in the 1980s: the library was renamed the William Frederic Badè Museum.

22. Carved inscriptions include: "Ye Shall Know The Truth, The Truth Shall Make You Free" (library entrance); "In Him Was Life And The Life Was The Light Of Men" (library fireplace); "Enter, Seek, Find, Go Forth To Give" (west entrance).

23. Alda Marsh Morgan, *From Ocean's Farthest Shore: The Church Divinity School of the Pacific's First One Hundred Years of Mission and Ministry* (Berkeley: CDSP, 1993), p. 36.

24. The school later purchased the entire triangular block bounded by Ridge Road, LeConte Avenue, and Euclid Avenue. Among the buildings acquired was the Tudoresque Alpha Delta Phi fraternity house, a post-fire work by Stafford Jory, at the hilltop juncture of Ridge Road and LeConte. The CDSP campus was largely rebuilt in the 1950s and 1960s. Gibbs Hall and All Saints' Chapel still stand. Ratcliff also designed a building for St. Margaret's House—the common name for the Deaconess Training School of the Pacific, which prepared women for positions within the Episcopal Church. The 1930 Spanish revivalist building, referred to variously as a "school" and "hotel" in published contracts, occupied a separate site at LeConte and Hearst Avenues, downhill from CDSP. *Daily Pacific Builder,* 28 Mar. 1930; 8 May 1930. The building is still standing.

25. Construction on the $39,000 building started in the fall of 1926, and the facility was dedicated in May 1927. *Building and Engineering News,* 27 Nov. 1926. Located at 2700 Bancroft Way, the building is still operated by the Presbyterian Church as a campus ministry. It was expanded in 2005 with a rear addition; at that time, the social hall was leased to a restaurant. Westminster House was designated a city landmark in 2000. Cerny, *Berkeley Landmarks,* p. 203.

26. "Hillside School was closed in 1980 and parts of the building are leased to several different educational institutions; currently it is not being well maintained." Cerny, *Berkeley Landmarks,* pp. 256–258. Located at 1581 LeRoy Avenue, at Buena Vista Way, the building is the most intact of Ratcliff's schools. It was designated a city landmark in 1980 and listed on the National Register of Historic Places in 1982. Ratcliff's other major school commission of the period, Cragmont School (1926), is no longer standing.

27. "The Berkeley Day Nursery was founded in 1908 as the first nursery for children of working parents in California. Following the influx of refugees from San Francisco after the 1906 earthquake, there was an urgent need for such a service. Members of the Berkeley Charities Organization, a group of public-spirited women, were its founders. The nursery was supported in its early years by private contributions and provided care for babies and young children, instruction in homemaking skills for older girls, vocational training for older boys,

and a day-work referral service." Cerny, *Berkeley Landmarks,* pp. 41–42. The building cost about $40,000 to build. *Daily Pacific Builder,* 11 June 1927. Located at 2031 Sixth Street, at Addison, it was sold to the Berkeley Unified School District in 1966 and subsequently leased for use as a community clinic. In 1977, the building was designated a city landmark and listed on the National Register of Historic Places.

28. *Building and Engineering News,* 20 Dec. 1924. The address of the house is 37 Roble Road. Edmond O'Neill was a retired professor of chemistry and former dean at the University of California. When Ratcliff studied chemistry as an undergraduate, he was O'Neill's assistant, helping the professor set up his experiments for lectures.

29. David Gebhard, "Life in the Dollhouse." In Sally Woodbridge, ed., *Bay Area Houses* (New York: Oxford University Press, 1976), pp. 104, 109–110. The Nayor residence, at 2 Somerset Place, was the only Ratcliff residence included in this study of the Bay Tradition. It was an expensive house, with a contract price of $30,000. *Daily Pacific Builder,* 19 Dec. 1925. Naylor was one of the downtown developers of the Chamber of Commerce Building.

30. The Blood residence, 1495 Euclid Avenue, had a listed contract price of $36,000, making it the architect's second costliest documented house. *Building and Engineering News,* 27 July 1929. Blood commissioned a second, less expensive house from Ratcliff at the same time; it was built nearby, on Hawthorne Terrace, probably for speculative purposes.

31. Two California architects, A. C. Schweinfurth of San Francisco and Irving Gill of San Diego, developed powerful and original styles within the Mission Revival movement. Gill enjoyed considerable success at first but his career languished after World War I. He was poised to receive the commission for the San Diego exposition before Goodhue, a better-known architect, lobbied for the job.

32. A variant name for the style is "Mediterranean."

33. California had a past, of course, an ancient human presence extending back thousands of years; it was the infant American culture enshrined at the Panama-California Exposition that had no past. Goodhue's use of colonial precedent for the exposition buildings was an appropriate image for a newly colonized state.

34. Robert Ratcliff recalled, "[My father] didn't travel very much. Traveling, for him, was not a thing of interest, really. As a matter of fact, he went to Europe that one time and he never went back . . . which my mother was unhappy about. . . . She never had been, and she never did go."

35. Also known as the Armstrong Schools of Business, this was one of Ratcliff's larger commissions of the early 1920s, built at a contract cost of $95,000. *Building and Engineering News,* 5 May 1923. Its exterior composition closely resembled Julia Morgan's 1906 library at Mills College, and the entire upper floor at the front retains a large open-truss hall. Berkeley's Judah L. Magnes Museum acquired the building in 2006. Located at 2222 Harold Way, it was designated a city landmark in 1994. Cerny, *Berkeley Landmarks,* pp. 256–258. In 1929, Ratcliff designed additions to the high school gymnasium on Milvia Street, doubling its size; after 1933, he undertook seismic upgrades and totally altered the exterior.

36. Other sources cite 1923 as the year of the appointment, e.g., Zoe A. Battu, "Historical and Architectural Highlights of Mills College," *Pacific Coast Architect,* Nov. 1928. The earlier date is from Richard Register and Paul Richards, *Proposal*

for a *Mills College Green Plan* (Oakland: Mills College Campus Facilities, 2004). This study includes an overview of campus development based on original drawings, documents, and photographs.

37. "Perhaps Maybeck thought Phoebe Hearst was about to foot the bill . . . He labeled his map 'Phoebe A. Hearst General Plan for Mills College.'" Register and Richards, *Proposal for a Mills College Green Plan,* p. 14.

38. In a few cases—the now-demolished Colonial Revival riding stables, a proposed neoclassical outdoor theater, and a proposed half-timbered English cottage for the Shakespeare Club—Ratcliff veered from Spanish revivalism. In each of these instances, the chosen style was particularly evocative of the program in terms of its historical associations.

39. "A Conversation with Peter Ratcliff, Son of Walter Ratcliff, Jr., Berkeley Architect." Interview conducted by Lesley Emmington, Anthony Bruce, and Don Craig of the Berkeley Architectural Heritage Society, Aug. 1997. Subsequent quotations from Peter Ratcliff are from this source.

40. Each of the eight wood posts has two carvings, on the front and back. The sixteen subjects are painters, sculptors, and architects from the Renaissance to the early twentieth century; no modernists were included. Two architects are depicted: the Englishman Christopher Wren and the American Charles McKim.

41. The complex was enlarged in the 1980s with harmonious additions by Esherick Homsey Dodge and Davis.

42. Built in 1901 on a creekside site at the center of the campus, Lisser Hall was a neoclassical wood-frame building with a colonnaded portico, by the short-lived partnership of George W. Percy and Willis Polk. Ratcliff remodeled the building in 1928 with stucco walls, tile roofs, and an arcaded portico, adding a classroom wing at the rear in 1938.

43. There are a total of fifteen frescoes in the auditorium—seven narrow frieze murals along each sidewall and one large mural on the stage backdrop—by the artist Ray Boynton.

44. Wetmore Gate is no longer in use, and the former entrance boulevard has been largely built over. Richards Gate, on MacArthur Boulevard (formerly Hopkins Street), currently serves as the sole public entrance to the campus.

45. Later called the Nell Ford Stone Clinic, the building was remodeled in 1968 to house the Mills College Children's School. It was sensitively rehabilitated and reopened in 2004 as the Vera Long Building for the Social Sciences.

46. The era of exclusive architectural posts with cities, counties, and campuses had largely ended by the 1940s. Arthur Brown, Jr., the last supervising architect at the University of California, resigned in 1948. His duties were taken over by campus officials who instituted the practice of hiring outside firms.

47. "Mills College Building Wins Honor Award," *San Francisco Chronicle,* 13 July 1929.

48. Rosalind A. Keep, "Plot and Plan at Mills College," *Architect and Engineer,* June 1932. Ratcliff's work was frequently published in the *Architect and Engineer* between 1924 and 1927, including a twenty-plate retrospective in Feb. 1926 ("Portfolio of Recent Work by W. H. Ratcliff, Jr."). A retrospective also appeared in the Nov. 1928 issue of *Pacific Coast Architect,* which featured the Music Building on its cover.

49. "Building, Loan Official Dies," *Berkeley Daily Gazette,* 8 Mar. 1940.

50. Under Ratcliff's management, Fidelity weathered the Depression and emerged after the war in excellent financial condition. During the worst years of the Depression, Fidelity did not foreclose on loans, but allowed borrowers to pay what they could. According to Peter Ratcliff, who went on to become Fidelity's president, the institution had one of the highest reserve ratios (a measure of financial soundness) of any California savings and loan when it was sold in 1961.

51. Biographical data on Haymond is from interviews with his daughter, Christine Kramer, conducted by the Ratcliff office (Christopher Ratcliff, Donald Crosby, and Elizabeth O'Hara) in Sept. 2002, and by the author in Jan. 2006. Further information provided by city directories and the obituary "Scott Coy Haymond," *Berkeley Gazette,* 22 Apr. 1976.

52. Late in his career, William Frederic Badè (1871–1936) became one of the pioneers of biblical archeology, leading six expeditions to Palestine between 1925 and 1935. He brought back thousands of artifacts to Berkeley. "Immediately after his return from his first exploratory trip, Professor Badè realized there was need for some permanent institute in which to house these important and extensive artifacts. . . . To that end, therefore, he believed that a Palestine Institute should be erected which would be dedicated to a serious and rigorous recovery of the 'lost' civilizations of the Ancient East. Only then could the church understand and reconstruct the social environment of peoples from whom the Biblical heritage comes. . . . In 1941, Mrs. Badè notified the Board of Trustees that she would present a William F. Badè Memorial to the Seminary, to fulfill in fact the dream of her late husband. A spacious building was erected on the northwest corner of the Administration Building to house the Palestine Institute . . . [It] was dedicated February 18, 1942, with the major address given by Professor Millar Burrows of Yale University." Hogue, *Christian Seed in Western Soil,* pp. 215–216.

The service station, commissioned by the Richfield Oil Co. in 1931, stands at 1952 Oxford Street; a Spanish revivalist complex with Moorish touches and fine brickwork, it was designated a city landmark in 1981. *Building and Engineering News,* 3 Jan. 1931; Cerny, *Berkeley Landmarks,* p. 119. The West Berkeley YMCA, 2009 Tenth Street, was designated a city "structure of merit" in 1992. Cerny, *Berkeley Landmarks,* p. 40. The English revivalist sorority, completed in 1937, is located at 2409 Warring Street. *Daily Pacific Builder,* 5 Oct. 1936.

53. Robert R. Weyeneth, "Merrill-Weyeneth House, Orinda, California" (Nomination to the National Register of Historic Places, July 2004). The house enclosed 6,000 square feet and cost at least $40,000 to build. Charles W. Merrill and George D. Blood were classmates in the College of Mining at UC Berkeley, both graduating in the early 1890s. Charles Merrill was an internationally known metallurgical engineer and businessman; he was a friend of Herbert Hoover. The Merrill residence was listed on the National Register in 2005—the first Ratcliff house so honored. It is possible that Scott Haymond was the designer, as the drawings are initialed "S.H." The Ratcliff office produced designs for two other houses in Orinda, including the 1937 Spanish-style residence of newly married Peter Ratcliff. In 1959, when he was president of Fidelity, Peter and his family moved into a modern house designed by his brother Robert; the new house was built next door to the Merrill residence. The Gulick residence is located at 3230 Storer Avenue, Oakland.

Chapter 4

1. Walter Ratcliff designed two ski lodges near Donner Pass: Sierra Ski Club, in the 1920s, and Clair Tappan Lodge, built by members of the Sierra Club in 1934 and 1935. Joel Hildebrand, "Ski Heil!," *Sierra Club Bulletin,* Feb. 1935.

2. Designed by John Galen Howard, the capacious building on Ridge Road—often cited as the largest shingled building in Berkeley—was built in 1904. It was one of relatively few Northside buildings to escape destruction in the 1923 fire.

3. "Rev. W. Ratcliff Dies in This City," *Berkeley Daily Gazette,* 31 Aug. 1925. His death occurred as the Pacific School of Religion was under construction. The widowed Evelyn Ratcliff continued to live at Cloyne Court until her death on February 24, 1942, shortly before her 88th birthday.

4. The family memory is that the commission for the Chamber of Commerce Building, in 1925, under-wrote the purchase of the ranch. In acquiring the retreat, Walter Ratcliff emulated William Frederic Badè, who owned a wooded tract of 160 acres in Napa County.

5. Designed by Howard, the building, now Northgate Hall, opened in 1906 and was enlarged multiple times. The school relocated to Wurster Hall in the 1960s.

6. These styles included Art Nouveau (New Art) in France and Belgium; Jugendstil (Youth Art) in Germany; Style Liberty (Free Art) in Italy; and Secessionism (Breakaway Art) in Austro-Hungary.

7. After 1910, Wright became widely known in Europe through German editions of his work.

8. When the Nazi government assumed power in 1933, one of its first actions was to shut down the Bauhaus, considered a center of decadent art. Breuer left Germany shortly before the fascist takeover; Gropius and Mies, soon after.

9. Schindler had worked for Wright, and he first came to Los Angeles in 1920 to supervise construction on Wright's Barnsdall residence, also known as the Hollyhock House. His friend Neutra arrived several years later.

10. Built near Santa Cruz, the Gregory farmhouse was seminal in many ways. On one level, it was a sophisticated work of revivalism, looking back to California's vernacular adobes and farmsteads for its formal inspiration and palette. On another level, it was a prototype for a new kind of single-family residence set level with the ground, adjoined by porches and patios, with flowing plans and simple finishes—the ubiquitous "ranch house," the successor to the bungalow and the dominant suburban house type in America from the 1930s to the 1960s. Finally, the play of the ensemble's horizontal and vertical rhythms, between the low wings and high tower, all residential in use, had a village-like quality that pointed forward to the equally seminal Sea Ranch condominium of the mid-1960s by Moore, Lyndon, Turnbull, Whitaker (MLTW). See Daniel Gregory, "William W. Wurster," in *Toward a Simpler Way of Life.*

11. Various terms have been used over the years, including "Bay Region Style," "Bay Area Tradition," and simply "Bay Tradition." Lewis Mumford coined the term "Bay Region Style" in a symposium at the Museum of Modern Art in New York, in 1948. The best overview of the tradition remains Sally Woodbridge, ed., *Bay Area Houses.*

12. Robert Paine (1870–1946) studied at the Chicago Art Institute and the Art Students League of New York, apprenticing under Augustus Saint-Gaudens. He first became known for his invention of a mechanical device that facilitated the enlargement

in scale of sculptures. Paine came to California to assist his friend A. Stirling Calder (the father of Alexander Calder) in the installation of statues and other sculptural pieces at the 1915 Panama-Pacific International Exposition in San Francisco. He was a mentor to Benny Bufano, a close family friend.

13. In his oral history, Robert Ratcliff stated that Scott Haymond was the principal designer and that the budget on the job was one million dollars. The $440,000 contract listed in *Daily Pacific Builder* (25 Sept. 1945) may have been for a portion of the job. In any event, it was the firm's largest single commission since the Chamber of Commerce Building in downtown Berkeley. Dinwiddie Construction Company rushed work on the job; the first rooms were occupied by students in October 1945. Fernwald was completed early in 1946. "Rooms with a View," *California Monthly*, Mar. 1947.

14. No longer extant, the two-story Hink Building was designed in 1923 by Walter Ratcliff.

15. Built and furnished for $85,000, Loper Chapel harmonized with existing buildings on the site: "Scott Haymond, the architect, designed the chapel in the New England colonial style used for the Sanctuary and Pilgrim Hall." James M. Spitze and Richard M. Eakin, *The Future Is Watching: A History of the First 125 Years of the First Congregational Church of Berkeley* (Berkeley: First Congregational Church of Berkeley, 1999). The chapel stands at the corner of Dana and Durant Avenues, a block south of the university campus.

16. Ratcliff faced similar resistance applying for a loan for his residence on Panoramic Way. "When I did my own house I had the same problem with these guys saying, 'You designed this crazy freak up on the hill there. How can we lend you money on that?!'" The postwar houses ranged in cost from $10,000 to $20,000 for smaller and earlier designs to as much as $100,000 for large and elaborate hillside residences. Relatively few cost more than $50,000.

17. "A House Steps Down a Steep Slope," *San Francisco Chronicle,* 10 Feb. 1952. The paper devoted a page to the house, with photographs by Rondal Partridge. The article noted how "angled rooms and overlapping roofs . . . helped orient, shade and dramatize the design. And the lack of doors let the house seem even more spacious than it is." The stepped design reprised features of Ratcliff's own residence. Frank Brezee built the house himself, finishing it in 1950. It is located at 2732 Shasta Road.

18. The Choate house is located at 401 Panoramic Way; the Culver house, at 929 Panoramic Way.

19. Located at 790 San Luis Road, the house cost around $100,000, making it one of Ratcliff's largest residential commissions. Dr. George M. Foster and his wife, Dr. Mary LeCron Foster, good friends of the Ratcliffs, were both noted anthropologists. He taught at UC Berkeley; she at CSU Hayward. Mrs. Foster recalled the day they moved into their house, in 1958: "We moved in in February, on one of those gusty days when it rains and then sun comes out for a few minutes. They were moving our furniture between gusts of rain, and the trees were whipping around. I'd never lived in a house with windows like this. It was the most exciting day of my life." Mary LeCron Foster, *Finding the Themes: Family, Anthropology, Language Origins, Peace and Conflict,* an oral history conducted in 2000 by Suzanne B. Riess, Regional Oral History Office, The Bancroft Library, University of California, Berkeley, 2001.

20. The American Baptist Seminary of the West is the only school in the Graduate Theological Union located south of the university campus. Had the

Berkeley Baptist Divinity School not recently invested in a building, it might well have followed the Pacific School of Religion and Church Divinity School of the Pacific to the Northside after the 1923 fire.

21. *Daily Pacific Builder,* 4 Aug. 1952, 2 Jan. 1953. The Baptist seminary jobs aggregated approximately $350,000 in construction. It is startling to realize that the ensemble dates from the 1950s; it could easily pass for the 1920s or 1930s. Ratcliff, Slama & Cadwalader sensitively added two more buildings to the complex in the 1960s.

22. The chapel was published: "Saint Margaret's Episcopal Chapel," *Architectural Record* (Dec. 1954).

23. Scott Haymond opened a one-man office in Berkeley and continued to practice until his retirement in 1964. His later work included Plymouth House (1956), a red-brick education building for the First Congregational Church, adjoining Loper Chapel. He died in Berkeley in 1976.

24. Ratcliff's arguments may have had some effect. The contract was first awarded to Ernest Born, a modernist whose design proved too daring. The accepted design, by Edward Powell of Los Angeles, was also modern. The aptly named Chapel of the Great Commission was dedicated May 8, 1956.

25. *Architect and Engineer,* Mar. 1958. The three-story sorority is at 2401 Piedmont Avenue, southeast corner of Channing Way. Walter Ratcliff's 1913 Shearman residence, at the other end of the block (2499 Piedmont Avenue), was altered for fraternity use around this time. The cited cost of $325,000 for the sorority constituted a large commission. Fraternity and sorority jobs were "bread and butter" for the firm in the 1950s and early 1960s. The office designed at least a

half-dozen new houses during these years, along with numerous alterations and additions.

26. Construction on the fire station began in the fall of 1959; it was completed in 1960. *Daily Pacific Builder,* 30 Oct. 1959. Jules Kliot is credited with the idea, though in final form the design was collaborative. "It was an interest ing building for us," said Robert Ratcliff. "It was interesting because it [was] the result of the coordinated work of all of us." Built at a cost of $115,000, the station occupied a triangular island fronting on The Alameda and bordered by Marin and Monterey Avenues—the site of the original Northbrae tract office.

Chapter 5

1. Charles Wollenberg, *Berkeley: A City in History,* ch. 8: "A Kind of Peace" (Berkeley: Berkeley Public Library, 2002), available at berkeleypubliclibrary.org.

2. In 1961, the directors of Fidelity Guaranty Savings and Loan (its name since 1952) agreed to sell the institution to a group of investors. Walter Ratcliff, who ended his career there as chairman of the board, had continued going into the office every day until it was sold, when he was 80. He divested the family's interest in the bank, distributing the proceeds among his children and grandchildren. In the forty years of his involvement with the bank, only one branch office had been opened, in Concord in the 1950s. Under its new ownership, renamed Fidelity Savings and Loan, the bank expanded to include dozens of branches. "From 1966, as Fidelity Savings and Loan, it expanded to about sixty offices around California. . . . In 1982 it was reorganized as part of Citicorp." Cerny, *Berkeley Landmarks,* p. 109.

3. In the 1960s, Berkeley was a world center of the lingering Arts and Crafts movement, as embodied in the evolving Bay Tradition. Charles Moore,

chairman of the architecture department at the College of Environmental Design from 1962 to 1965, was its most significant figure. The firm of Moore, Lyndon, Turnbull, Whitaker (MLTW) came to prominence with the Sea Ranch Condominium (1965), a seminal work of wood-clad, vernacular modernism that provided a vocabulary for apartments and condo complexes across the country. Sea Ranch was the third major export of the California Arts and Crafts movement, after the bungalow and the ranch house. See Roger Montgomery, "Mass Producing Bay Area Architecture," in Sally Woodbridge, ed., *Bay Area Houses.*

4. The brick building, which Robert Ratcliff purchased, literally straddled the border, giving the firm the ability to claim residency in either city. "We had two addresses and two business licenses and were in line for municipal work in both cities," Cadwalader recalled. The addresses were 3408 Grove Street, Berkeley, and 6117 Grove Street, Oakland. Shortly after the move, Bay Area Rapid Transit (BART) acquired a portion of the property as right of way for its elevated train tracks on Grove Street; the compensation helped the firm upgrade the remnant of the warehouse with a courtyard and other amenities.

5. The most recent edition, edited by John Raeber, is the *Construction Inspection Manual,* 7th ed. (Los Angeles: BNI Building News, 1998).

6. *Ratcliff: The Living Firm,* comp. Don Crosby (in-house publication, 2000). All subsequent quotations from Ratcliff personnel are from this source or previously cited interviews. Jules Kliot was another non-UCB architect who played a significant, albeit short-term, design role within the firm; he received his B.A. in architecture from the University of Michigan.

7. Despite its metropolitan stature, the Bay Area remained a largely Balkanized region with many competing jurisdictions and few exemplars of unified action. The architectural profession reflected this parochialism to some degree and the traditional population centers of San Francisco, Oakland, and San Jose tended to be bailiwicks of long-established firms.

8. Don Kasamoto and Peter Scott were both brought into the firm to work on this project. The pavilion plan, Wrightian hexagons, and predilection for wood were signature motifs of Burns Cadwalader. Located on San Pablo Avenue, the shopping center was razed in the 1980s.

9. Established in 1950 as a successor to Russell de Lappe, a prolific designer of city halls and courthouses, the firm is now known as VBN.

10. When Oakland became the county seat in the 1870s, a courthouse and hall of records were erected on Broadway. Rendered obsolete by the new courthouse on Lake Merritt, the landmarks were cut off from the downtown by the Eastshore Freeway (now I-880) after World War II. The courthouse was demolished in 1950; the hall of records in 1964.

11. Multistory parking structures were in fact a distinctive new building type in American cities, symbols of the postwar culture.

12. The $11-million construction contract for this job was the largest yet for the firm.

13. An office précis outlined the program: "Phase I Expansion Project: New construction housing the Central Logistics System, Pharmacy/Ostomy Department, Radiology, Surgery, Nuclear Medicine, Clinical Lab, and Physical Therapy; Consolidated Obstetrics Center housing labor/delivery, a 32-bed postpartum care unit with family-centered maternity care program, a 32-bed bassinet normal-newborn nursery, and an 8-bed neonatal intensive care unit."

14. The concrete fireplace, with angled base and lofty flue, was one of his largest, and strangest. It resembled a rocket ship ready to be launched from its wood pad, suggesting that the Arts and Crafts aesthetic had reached its outer limits.

15. The Oakland building was featured on the cover of the July 1967 issue of *Architect & Contractor,* an Oakland trade journal. Murray Slama collaborated on the design of the Berkeley office.

16. First opened in 1965, UC Santa Cruz was the ninth campus of the statewide university system, and the last to be established in two decades of postwar expansion. The tenth campus, UC Merced, opened in 2005.

17. Ratcliff collaborated on the design with another architect in the firm, Sandy Pollock.

18. Situated at the northeast corner of Shattuck and Durant Avenues, the bank and parking lot replaced two buildings by Walter Ratcliff—his fine Fire Station No. 2 (1914) and the Lester Hink Building (1923), where the firm had its offices after World War II. The three-part symmetry of the Bank of California echoed the façade of Ratcliff's Fidelity Building (1926), two doors to the north. This was Jules Kliot's last design for the firm. He remained in Berkeley, where he became a conceptual artist, started his own weaving equipment business, and with his wife, Kaethe, founded the Lacis Museum of Lace and Textiles.

19. The AAA office is located at 1775 University Avenue, near Grant Street.

20. One of these projects began in the late 1950s under Ratcliff & Ratcliff. Since the 1970s, the three buildings have housed the College of Natural Resources.

21. In 2005, USCA had twenty facilities in the vicinity of the campus, housing over thirteen hundred students. The Ridge Project (now Casa Zimbabwe) was described in a recent USCA brochure:

"Inside this stucco-frosted building on the Northside of campus lies a small village of happily diverse students who study, relax, and foster creativity in one another with enough space to let the social and the private coexist peacefully. A big, beautiful rooftop area with a stunning view of the entire bay area is but the icing on this cake."

22. The project was never built, and People's Park remains undeveloped. The bullet hole stayed in the office's front window, which was not replaced.

23. Now known as Rochdale Village (1971) and Fenwick Weavers' Village (1981), the complex's nine buildings contain 132 units with a capacity of 361 students.

24. "Walter Ratcliff Dies—He Helped Shape the City," *Berkeley Gazette,* 8 May 1973.

Chapter 6

1. "The College [of Environmental Design] was created in 1959 under Dean William Wilson Wurster to administratively link Architecture, which had outgrown the Ark. . . . Landscape Architecture, which was still part of the College of Agriculture . . . and City and Regional Planning. . . . Wurster called upon four members of his Architecture faculty—Vernon DeMars, Joseph Esherick, Donald Olsen, and Donald Hardison—to design the state-funded Environmental Design building." Harvey Helfand, *The Campus Guide: University of California, Berkeley,* pp. 215-216. The building was intended as an architectonic laboratory where students could observe exposed structural and mechanical systems firsthand; its "unfinished" quality would serve as a neutral backdrop for student work. The building's visual boldness owed much to the sculptural aesthetic of raw-concrete Brutalism (*concret brut,* Fr.).

2. Alexander's ideas were first disseminated by the

Center for Environmental Structure, Berkeley, in *A Pattern Language Which Generates Multi-Service Centers* (with Sara Ishikawa and Murray Silverstein, 1968) and *Houses Generated by Patterns* (Christopher Alexander with Sanford Hirshen, Sara Ishikawa, Christie Coffin, 1969). The better-known version was published (with Sara Ishikawa and Murray Silverstein) as Christopher Alexander, *A Pattern Language: Towns, Buildings, Construction* (New York: Oxford University Press, 1977).

3. Named for a former president of the university, this annual award was the business community's equivalent of an Oscar for Lifetime Achievement.

4. The graphic designer Michael Manwaring was retained to design the office's brochures, mailers, stationery, and business cards.

5. The number of passengers flying in and out of these airports would double over the following decade and a half, totaling about sixty million by the year 2000.

6. Allan Temko, "Oakland's New Airport Terminal Is Simply Splendid," *San Francisco Chronicle,* 18 May 1985. Temko, who died in 2006, received the 1990 Pulitzer Prize for criticism.

7. Elmwood Village is located at 2980 College Avenue, not far from Walter Ratcliff's 1925 Mercantile Bank.

8. Covering about seventy acres, Arrowhead Marsh is the last remnant of some two thousand acres of marshland that once encompassed San Leandro Bay. The marsh forms part of the 1,220-acre Martin Luther King, Jr., Regional Shoreline, which is administered by the East Bay Regional Park District on land partially leased from the Port of Oakland. See Woodruff Minor, *Pacific Gateway: An Illustrated History of the Port of Oakland* (Oakland: Port of Oakland, 2000), pp. 160–161.

9. Now known as the Department of Veterans Affairs.

10. Maglaty went on to work for Esherick Homsey Dodge and Davis.

11. The University of Oregon hired Christopher Alexander to help plan campus development. It was the first major experimental application of pattern language, and the results were published by Alexander (with Denny Abrams, Shlomo Angel, Sara Ishikawa, and Murray Silverstein) in *The Oregon Experiment* (New York: Oxford University Press, 1975).

12. The Chemical and Physical Sciences Facility at UC Santa Barbara was a Ratcliff project that ended up being designed by Robert Stern. The two firms were not formally associated on the job.

13. BAHA's fifth annual tour, in 1980, was entitled "The Residential Work in Berkeley of Walter H. Ratcliff, Jr." Previous tours focused on the buildings of Julia Morgan (1976), John Galen Howard (1977), Ernest Coxhead (1978), and Henry Higby Gutterson (1979). In recognition of the firm's centennial, BAHA sponsored a second tour of Walter Ratcliff houses in 2006.

14. Projects included a Historic Structures Report for the John Marsh House, in Contra Costa County, and a contract to reconstruct historic structures at Fort Vancouver, Washington. Slama also authored a booklet on the subject, *Historic Structures Preservation Guide,* for the National Park Service.

15. Ratcliff did further work on the building in the 1990s, after it sustained damage in the 1989 Loma Prieta earthquake.

Chapter 7

1. See Arie de Geus, *The Living Company: Habits for Survival in a Turbulent Business Environment* (Cambridge, Mass.: Harvard Business School, 1997). This study of longevity among companies is one of Kit Ratcliff's favorite books.

2. The seven were Stephanie Bartos, Norma Bower, Crodd Chin, Carl Christensen, Christie Coffin, Kava Massih, and Brad Neal. Massih left the firm in 1996 to start his own practice in Berkeley.

3. In *Ratcliff: The Living Firm,* p. 83.

4. Don Crosby retired in 2002, when he turned 65. Dan Wetherell, an architect who joined the firm in 1986, was made associate principal in 2001 and COO and principal in 2005.

5. For his contributions to the field, Husain was made a Fellow of the American Institute of Architects (FAIA). Murray Slama was also so honored.

6. Designed by MBT Associates and completed in 1988 on the west side of the building, the Life Sciences Addition houses forty-three laboratories as well as containment areas for animals used in research. Its façades and roof treatment were contextually sensitive, but its bulk (six stories, 300 feet long) impinged on axial sightlines, upset existing symmetries, and towered over the historic eucalyptus grove by the campus's west entrance. Helfand, *The Campus Guide: University of California, Berkeley,* pp. 147–152.

7. The facility was renamed the Valley Life Sciences Building in honor of its principal donor.

8. Helfand, *The Campus Guide: University of California, Berkeley,* pp. 242–245.

9. Helfand, *The Campus Guide: University of California, Berkeley,* pp. 63–64.

10. After the Anna Head School for Girls relocated to Oakland in 1964, the affiliated Josiah Royce School for Boys was opened on an adjoining site; the two schools merged in 1979 to form Head-Royce, a coeducational preparatory school that had 750 K–12 students in 2005.

11. For a discussion of the ambiguities of the term "nature" in architecture, see chapter 3, "Nature," in Dell Upton, *Oxford History of Art: Architecture in the United States* (Oxford and New York: Oxford University Press, 1998).

Suggested Reading

This short list of selected source material is recommended for those wishing to delve further into themes treated in this book. General surveys of architecture and history are not included.

Boutelle, Sara Holmes. *Julia Morgan, Architect* (New York: Abbeville Publishers, 1995. Originally published in 1988).

Cardwell, Kenneth H. *Bernard Maybeck: Artisan, Architect, Artist* (Santa Barbara and Salt Lake City: Peregrine Smith, Inc., 1977).

Cerny, Susan Dinkelspiel. *Berkeley Landmarks* (Berkeley: Berkeley Architectural Heritage Association, 2001).

Corbett, Michael R. *Splendid Survivors: San Francisco's Downtown Architectural Heritage* (San Francisco: California Living Books, 1979).

de Geus, Arie. *The Living Company: Habits for Survival in a Turbulent Business Environment* (Boston: Harvard Business School Press, 2002. Originally published in 1997).

Helfand, Harvey. *The Campus Guide: University of California, Berkeley* (New York: Princeton Architectural Press, 2002).

Longstreth, Richard. *On the Edge of the World: Four Architects in San Francisco at the Turn of the Century* (New York: The Architectural History Foundation; Cambridge, Mass., and London: MIT Press, 1983).

McCoy, Esther. *Five California Architects* (New York: Praeger Publishers, 1975. Originally published in 1960).

Winter, Robert W., ed. *Toward a Simpler Way of Life: The Arts & Crafts Architects of California* (Berkeley, Los Angeles, and London: University of California Press, 1997).

Woodbridge, Sally, ed. *Bay Area Houses* (New York: Oxford University Press, 1976).

Woodbridge, Sally B. *John Galen Howard and the University of California: The Design of a Great Public University Campus* (Berkeley, Los Angeles, and London: University of California Press, 2002).

Illustration Credits

Index

HEYDAY INSTITUTE

Since its founding in 1974, Heyday Books has occupied a unique niche in the publishing world, specializing in books that foster an understanding of the history, literature, art, environment, social issues, and culture of California and the West. We are a 501(c)(3) nonprofit organization based in Berkeley, California, serving a wide range of people and audiences.

We are grateful for the generous funding we've received for our publications and programs during the past year from foundations and more than 300 individual donors. Major supporters include:

Anonymous; Anthony Andreas, Jr., Arroyo Fund; Barnes & Noble bookstores; Bay Tree Fund; S.D. Bechtel, Jr. Foundation; California Oak Foundation; Candelaria Fund; Columbia Foundation; Colusa Indian Community Council; Wallace Alexander Gerbode Foundation; Richard & Rhoda Goldman Fund; Evelyn & Walter Haas, Jr. Fund; Walter & Elise Haas Fund; Hopland Band of Pomo Indians; James Irvine Foundation; Guy Lampard & Suzanne Badenhoop; Jeff Lustig; George Frederick Jewett Foundation; LEF Foundation; David Mas Masumoto; James McClatchy; Michael McCone; Gordon & Betty Moore Foundation; Morongo Band of Mission Indians; National Endowment for the Arts; National Park Service; Poets & Writers; Rim of the World Interpretive Association; River Rock Casino; Alan Rosenus; San Francisco Foundation; John-Austin Saviano/Moore Foundation; Sandy Cold Shapero; Ernest & June Siva; L.J. Skaggs and Mary C. Skaggs Foundation; Swinerton Family Fund; Susan Swig Watkins; and the Harold & Alma White Memorial Fund.

For more information about Heyday Institute, our publications and programs, please visit our website at www.heydaybooks.com.

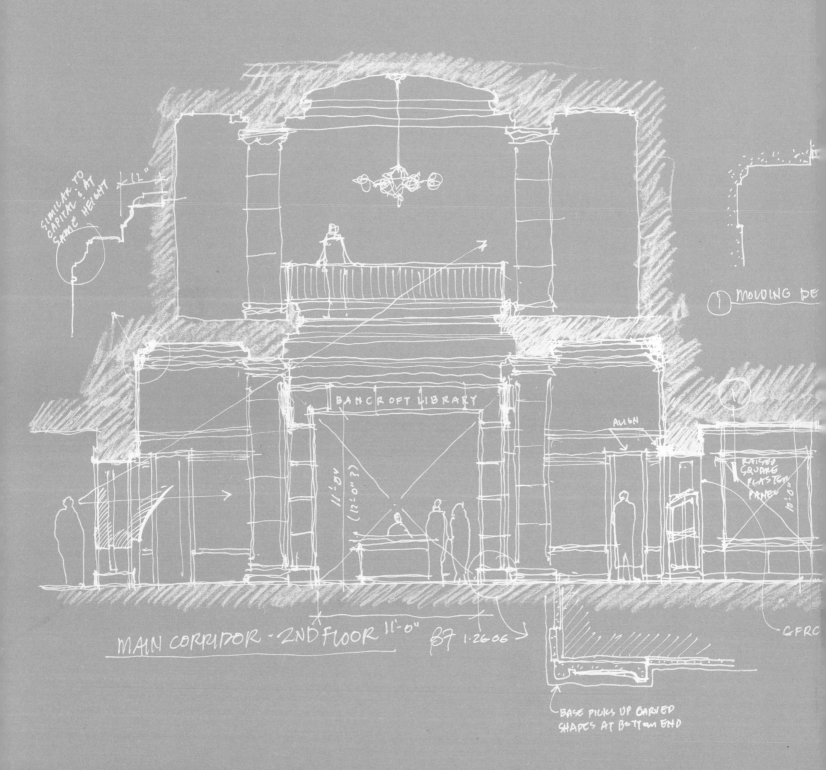

SIMILAR TO
CAPITAL : AT
SAME HEIGHT

11"

MOULDING DE

BANCROFT LIBRARY

ALIGN

11'-0"
(12'-0"?)

RAISED
SQUARE
PLASTER
PANEL

GFRC

MAIN CORRIDOR - 2ND FLOOR 11'-0" BT 1-26-06

BASE PICKS UP CARVED
SHAPES AT BOTTOM END